The Apprentice Fiction of

F. SCOTT FITZGERALD

1909–1917

The Apprentice Fiction of
F. SCOTT FITZGERALD
1909–1917

Edited with an introduction by JOHN KUEHL

Rutgers University Press

New Brunswick   *New Jersey*

The stories are reprinted here with permission of Mrs. Samuel J.
Lanahan.

Quotations from *Scott Fitzgerald*, by Andrew Turnbull (copyright © 1962 by Andrew Turnbull), and *The Letters of F. Scott Fitzgerald*, edited by Andrew Turnbull (copyright © 1963 by Frances Scott Fitzgerald Lanahan), are reprinted here with permission of Charles Scribner's Sons.

Contents

Preface

Among The F. Scott Fitzgerald Papers in the Department of Rare Books and Special Collections at The Princeton University Library there are two small red-bound scrapbooks. The one entitled "Other Contributions of Scott Fitzgerald to School and College Magazines 1909-1919" contains tearsheets of all the author's prep-school publications. This and the other, which is entitled "Various Contributions of Scott Fitzgerald To the Nassau Literary Magazine of Princeton 1915-1917," contain tearsheets of all his college publications except musical comedy lyrics and material printed in *The Princeton Tiger*. Extensive investigation has failed to uncover a run of the Newman School *News* during 1912-1913, but since the St. Paul Academy's broken run of the *Now and Then* during 1909-1911 and Princeton University's complete run of *The Nassau Literary Magazine* during 1913-1917 include no additional stories, it is assumed that Fitzgerald, who was always a great saver, did not publish any stories at Newman that he neglected to preserve.

The apprentice fiction appears here *exactly* the way these magazines printed it—typographical errors and all—for essentially two reasons: to obviate the necessity on the reader's part of examining nearly inaccessible documents in order to determine precisely the original printed texts of Fitzgerald's prep-school and college stories; to obviate the necessity on the editor's part of entering that treacherous world of emendations where so many arbitrary decisions must be made. Quotations—which, whenever possible, come from unpublished or hard-to-obtain documents—also appear here *exactly* as they do in their sources. Although the book is organized along straightforward chronological lines, not all of the *Now and*

Then and *Newman News* stories have been given separate intro-
ductions, and although one-act plays have been included, parodies
have not.

I wish to thank Fitzgerald's daughter, Mrs. Samuel J. Lanahan,
for granting me permission to publish her father's previously un-
collected apprentice fiction, and Princeton University for provid-
ing generously from its Research Fund. Mr. Alexander P. Clark
and Mrs. Alden Randall of The Princeton University Library rendered especially valuable assistance. Helpful too were Mr. Matthew
J. Bruccoli, Mr. James B. Merod, Mr. John T. Corry, the Very
Reverend Monsignor Henry G. J. Beck, and Miss Dorothy Olding.

JOHN KUEHL

Princeton, N.J.
November, 1964

The Apprentice Fiction of

F. SCOTT FITZGERALD

1909–1917

Introduction

An unpublished autobiography marked "Outline Chart of My Life," but commonly called "Ledger" (The F. Scott Fitzgerald Papers, Princeton University Library), shows Scott Fitzgerald to have been an actor from the age of seven: "He remembers the attic where he had a red sash with which he acted Paul Revere" (September, 1903); "He made up shows in Ingham's attic, all based on the American Revolution and a red sash and three cornered hat. He did tricks and mysteriously vanished a dime" (September, 1906); "His mother got the idea he could sing so he performed 'Way down in colon town' and 'Don't get married anymore' for all visitors" (January, 1907). Besides writing four plays between the summer of 1911 and the summer of 1914 for the local Elizabethan Dramatic Club, he played the lead in two and important parts in both of the others.

If, like Dick Diver (*Tender Is the Night*, New York, 1934), Scott Fitzgerald felt compelled to perform, like Jay Gatsby (*The Great Gatsby*, New York, 1925), he also undertook proprietary roles. For instance, his childhood diary, "Thoughtbook" (The F. Scott Fitzgerald Papers), contains a section dated February 24, 1911, and entitled "The gooserah and other clubs," which informs us that the author originated "the gooserah club" and helped to originate "the white handkerchief club." "Thoughtbook," itself, would serve as the source of Basil Duke Lee's "Book of Scandal," just as the title of one of the Basil Duke Lee stories, "The Scandal Detectives" (*Taps at Reveille*, New York, 1935) would recall an actual organization of this name founded—probably by Fitzgerald—in March, 1911.

Most important, however, like Monroe Stahr (*The Last Tycoon*, New York, 1941), who would guide motion pictures "way up past the range and power of the theatre," Fitzgerald entertained in the role of creative artist. Scott Fitzgerald was a born storyteller. One early piece states, "It is because of Skiggs that this story was written," and another, "It is unfortunately one of those stories which must start at the beginning, and the beginning consists merely of a few details." We do not require his frequent consciousness of himself as a writer, though, to realize that he thoroughly enjoyed entertaining his readers. In his apprentice fiction Fitzgerald employed dramatic beginnings, surprise endings, and lively scenes. He chose exciting subjects: solving a murder mystery; winning a football game single-handedly; an act of physical courage in the Civil War; avenging the murder of a son after the Civil War; giving away money on Christmas Eve; doing unto a Christian Scientist what he has done unto you; searching futilely for a nobleman; rediscovering a father; overcoming doubt before joining the Jesuits; the debut of a *femme fatale*; regret at having flunked out of college; Shakespeare raping Lucrece's "real-life" model, then composing a poem about it; a boy's attempt to kiss a fickle girl; demoralization and death during World War I; a man finally winning an old flame only to lose his writing ability.

He presented these subjects with considerable narrative sense, as a brief summary of one story's action will indicate. "The Pierian Springs and the Last Straw" contains two parts. The opening section of the long first part elaborates the statement, "My Uncle George assumed, during my childhood, almost legendary proportions"; he drank heavily and was a "mesogamist" who "had been engaged seven times" and "had written a series of novels" about bad or not quite good women. The closing section takes the narrator—now a twenty-year-old easterner—to "the prosperous Western city that still supported the roots of our family tree," where, in the Iroquois Club, his uncle explains why his life stopped "at sixteen minutes after ten" one October evening. For an entire decade he has put up with the ridicule of the woman responsible, but on the present occasion she grows unbearably sarcastic. When she says she often talked her dead husband out of horsewhipping him, George stamps her wedding ring into "a beaten button of gold." Then Part I ends and the nephew departs. A couple of short paragraphs, Part II describes the uncle's fate while implying the nephew's relation to it. We learn that the older man and the widow soon eloped, with the result that he "never drank again, nor did he ever write or in fact do anything except play a middling amount of golf and get comfortably bored with his wife." The nephew's awareness of storytelling is illustrated by such comments as "The story ought to end here" and "Unfortunately the play continues into an inartistic sixth act." His last assertions refer facetiously to "my new book on *Theories of Genius*," so we feel that he may become the family author, and if he does, will probably continue to exploit Scott Fitzgerald's own budding gift for irony.

II

The "Thoughtbook," whose dated entries extend from August, 1910, to February 24, 1911, shows that Fitzgerald was a born storyteller even in the keeping of a diary. That at the age of fourteen he had already developed the raconteur's sense of time is indicated through his juxtaposing the definite past, the indefinite past, and the present. That he dramatized factual events is shown by many episodes that focus on a memorable day and that contain stretches of direct dialogue.

> "Jim was so confident the other night that you had a crush on him."
> "Well Jim gets another think"
> "Shall I let him know you dont like him."
> "No: but you can let him know that he isn't first."
> "Ill do that"
> "Now if you had thought that it might be different."
> "Good" said I
> "Good" repeated she and then the convestion lagged.

"Thoughtbook" also reveals that Fitzgerald was a born psychologist. He characterized two of his friends thus: Paul Ballion "was awfully funny, strong as an ox; cool in the face of danger polite and at times very interesting." Margaret Armstrong "is not pretty but I think she is very attractive looking. She is extremly graceful and a very good dancer and the most interesting talker I have ever seen or heard." He recorded other people's reactions to him: "Violets' opinean of my character was that I was polite and had a nice disposition and that I thought I was the whole push and that I got mad too easily." And his reactions to other people: "Bob Clark is interesting to talk to because he lets me do a lot of talking"; "Now I dont dislike him [Paul Ballion]. I have simply out grown him"; "I think it is charming to hear her [Margaret Armstrong] say, 'Give it to me as a compliment' when I tell her I have a trade."

C. N. B. Wheeler, English teacher and athletic coach, has described the Scott Fitzgerald of St. Paul (Minnesota) Academy days (1908-1911) as a psychologist as well as an entertainer: "a sunny light-haired boy full of enthusiasm who fully foresaw his course in life even in his schoolboy days. . . . I helped him by encouraging his urge to write adventures. It was his best work, he did not shine in his other subjects. He was inventive in all playlets we had and marked his course by his pieces for delivery before the school. . . . He wasn't popular with his schoolmates. He saw through them too much and wrote about it. . . . I imagined he would become an actor of the variety type, but he didn't. . . . It was his pride in his literary work that put him in his real bent." (Andrew Turnbull, *Scott Fitzgerald*, New York, 1962, p. 20)

Fitzgerald's precocity as an observer of human character is foreshadowed in the four stories written for the St. Paul Academy *Now and Then*. The main figures of the first two, both of whom are handicapped, act heroically but under rather conventional circumstances: the "pretty light" substitute halfback, Reade, and the "wounded" Confederate private, Jack Sanderson, vanquish their respective football and battlefield foes and earn cheers from their comrades.

In the other two *Now and Then* stories, the characters are

either passive or active. A mystery confronts two pairs of men, but while the observers, Chief Egan and Robert Calvin Raymond, record, the observed, John Syrel and Governor Carmatle, act. This passage implies Chief Egan's envy of John Syrel: "He was not a tall man, but thanks to the erectness of his posture, and the suppleness of his movement, it would take no athlete to tell that he was of fine build. He was twenty-three years old when I first saw him, and was already a reporter on the News. He was not a handsome man: his face was clean-shaven, and his chin showed him to be of strong character."

The protagonists of all three stories Scott Fitzgerald published during his residence at the Newman School of Hackensack, New Jersey (1911-1913), combine both active and passive traits. But the author's assessment of the protagonists' experience in two early Princeton pieces, "Shadow Laurels" and "The Ordeal," is even more complex. Although they overcome their difficulties, they do so less successfully than the protagonists of the three Newman School stories.

In "Shadow Laurels" Jacques Chandelle, whose "eyes are clear and penetrating," whose chin "is sharp and decisive," and whose manner "is that of a man accustomed only to success," feels the need after a separation of twenty-eight years to "sense" his father again. This he does, thanks to some of the deceased's old Parisian cronies. Discovering through them that Chandelle senior was a magnificent failure, Jacques begins to metamorphose into him: "His face is a little red and his hand unsteady. He appears infinitely more gallic than when he entered the wine shop." As the son departs, one old crony shouts the father's name, "Jean, Jean, don't go—don't." The young man of "The Ordeal," to whom "pleasure, travel, the law, the diplomatic service" are open, is, nevertheless, about to take religious vows. Yet the very day he must file toward the altar with the other novices, he finds himself "pitted against an infinity of temptation."

The protagonists of "Shadow Laurels" and "The Ordeal" triumph only ostensibly. Jacques Chandelle and the young man accomplish what they set out to do, the former managing to rediscover his father and the latter managing to go through with his religious vows, but both contain the seeds of failure. "Shadow Laurels" implies that Jacques Chandelle is more like his reprobate father than he imagines, and "The Ordeal" shows that the young man's faith has been preserved only through an external force— "the stained window of St. Francis Xavier." These two 1915 stories represent, then, an interim stage in the development of the author's hero.

In "The Spire and the Gargoyle," which was written two years later, the hero flunks an *actual* test. No previous Fitzgerald protagonist had failed completely. In this case, the boy has to a very large extent brought his failure about himself: "Fifty cut recitations in his first wild term had made necessary the extra course of which he had just taken the examination. Winter muses, unacademic and cloistered by Forty-second Street and Broadway, had stolen hours from the dreary stretches of February and March. Later, time had crept insidiously through the lazy April afternoons and seemed so intangible in the long Spring twilights. So June found him unprepared."

Total failure on the part of the main figures of subsequent Princeton pieces had been prefigured as early as the *Now and Then* stories, where the heroes were handicapped or fragmented into actors and passive observers. Inevitably, Scott Fitzgerald's juvenile protagonist, through personal weakness or some external force or both, would become the *homme manqué*, a term Fitzgerald himself would use to describe Dick Diver.

This evolution involved sex. In "The Ordeal," the young man's worldly temptation is epitomized by a female, "waiting, ever waiting": "He saw struggles and wars, banners waving somewhere, voices giving hail to a king—and looking at him through it all were the sweet sad eyes of the girl who was now a woman." In "Sentiment—and the Use of Rouge," Clay Syneforth, twenty-two years old and "champion of sentiment," comes home after two years of war to find the girls' heavily painted faces expressing "half enthusiasm and half recklessness." Just before Syneforth and his dead brother's fiancée sleep together, "He put his arm around her, never once taking his eyes from her face, and suddenly the whole strength of her appeal burst upon him. . . . He knew what was wrong, but he knew also that he wanted this woman, this warm creature of silk and life who crept so close to him. There were reasons why he oughtn't to have her."

Speaking of *la belle dame sans merci*, Mario Praz has written: "*Salammbô* is a picture in the manner of Delacroix, except that instead of the beautiful female slaves agonizing under the ferocious eye of Sardanapalus, we have the beautiful male slave suffering unspeakable tortures under the eye of his goddess-like beloved; for with Flaubert we have entered the dominion of the Fatal Woman, and sadism appears under the passive aspect which is usually called masochism (as though the active and passive aspects were not usually both present in sadism, and a mere change of proportions really justified a change of name)." (*The Romantic Agony*, New York, 1956, pp. 153-4)

After the *homme manqué*, the *femme fatale*, Fitzgerald's vampiric destroyer, is the most vital character he ever created. She pervades the later fiction. For instance, Jonquil of "The Sensible Thing," Judy of "Winter Dreams," and Josephine of the five Josephine stories surround themselves with devoted males whom they seem to delight in torturing with uncertainty. Josephine "had driven mature men to a state of disequilibrium" (*Taps at Reveille*, p. 178) and Judy was destined to "bring no end of misery to a great number of men." (*All the Sad Young Men*, New York, 1926, p. 59) Another young lady, Ailie Calhoun of "The Last of the Belles," was proud of the fact that a man may have committed suicide over her. (*Taps at Reveille*, p. 260) But more pertinently, the *femme fatale* pervades the apprentice fiction too. From the heroine of "A Luckless Santa Claus" (Christmas, 1912) to the heroine of "The Pierian Springs and the Last Straw" (October, 1917), she acts as the most persistent and powerful barrier to the protagonist's success. The *femme fatale* is no mere foil, however. Her development into an independently significant figure represents one of the major achievements of these early writings, whose author told his secretary, "I am half feminine—at least my

mind is. . . . Even my feminine characters are feminine Scott
Fitzgeralds." (*Scott Fitzgerald*, p. 259)

That Fitzgerald's conception of the *femme fatale* was inti-
mately bound up with personal experience seems clear from statements like this to his daughter: "When I was your age I lived with
a great dream. The dream grew and I learned how to speak of it
and make people listen. Then the dream divided one day when
I decided to marry your mother after all, even though I knew she
was spoiled and meant no good to me. I was sorry immediately
I had married her but, being patient in those days, made the best
of it and got to love her in another way. You came along and
for a long time we made quite a lot of happiness out of our lives.
But I was a man divided—she wanted me to work too much for
her and not enough for my dream." (Andrew Turnbull [ed.],
The Letters of F. Scott Fitzgerald, New York, 1963, p. 32) Actually, Fitzgerald had been associated with strong-willed females
before marrying Zelda Sayre.

His mother, Mary McQuillan, was the daughter of an Irish immigrant who had prospered in St. Paul as a wholesale grocer.
There were many things he resented about her, among them that
she had taste neither in dress nor in books and that she was over-
indulgent. In an article called "Author's House" (*Esquire*, July,
1936), Fitzgerald indicates that her overindulgence was responsible for his choosing the passive life of an artist rather than a
more active, more "heroic" life. He conducts an anonymous visitor
to his cellar, where there is "all the complicated dark mixture of
my youth and infancy that made me a fiction writer instead of a
fireman or a soldier," and, pointing to the darkest corner, he says:
"Three months before I was born my mother lost her other two
children and I think that came first of all though I don't know
how it worked exactly. I think I started then to be a writer." All
his life Fitzgerald felt that his mother had made him soft rather
than strong, had kept him from becoming the "hero" his fantasy
wished him to be.

Regardless of whether or not Mary McQuillan should bear the
ultimate responsibility for her son's preoccupation with the *femme*

fatale, there is no denying that from childhood through marriage this kind of female fascinated him. At eleven, he found Kiddy Williams irresistible: "I dont remember who was first but I know that Earl was second and as I was already quite over come by her charms I then and there resolved that I would gain first place . . . We talked and talked and finally she asked me if I was going to Robin's party and it was there my eventful day was. We played postoffice, pillow, clapp in and clapp out and other foolish but interesting games. It was impossible to count the number of times I kissed Kitty that afternoon. At any rate when we went home I had secured the coveted 1st place. I held this until dancing school stopped in the spring and then relinquished it to Johnny Gowns a rival. On valentines day that year Kitty recieved no less than eighty four valentines."

"Thoughtbook" records another childish affair immediately succeeding this one, the new *belle dame sans merci* being Violet Stockton: "She was very pretty with dark brown hair and eyes big and soft. She spoke with a soft southern accent leaving out the r's. She was a year older than I but together with most of the other boys liked her very much. I met her through Jack Mitchell who lived next door to her. He himself was very attached as was Art Foley. . . . Finally Violet had a party which was very nice and it was the day after this that we had the quarrel. She had some sort of a book called flirting by sighns and Jack and I got it away from Violet and showed it too all the boys. Violet got very mad and therefor I went home. . . . *I just hate Violet*. . . . Not much has happened since Violet went away. The day she went away was my birthday and she gave me a box of candy. Her latest fancy is Arthur Foley. He has her ring She wrote him a letter to ask him for his picture"

Fitzgerald's "Ledger" records his college romance with Ginevra King in a series of short statements whose very matter-of-factness lends them poignancy: January, 1915: "Met Ginevra"; June: "Ritz, Nobody Home and Midnight Folie with Ginevra. . . . Deering: I'm going to take Ginevra home in my electric"; August: "No news from Ginevra"; October: "Dinner with Ginevra in

Waterbury"; November: "Letters to G.K."; February, 1916: "Long
letters to Ginevra"; March: "Ginevra fired from school"; April:
"Ginevra & Living on the train. A facinating story"; August:
"Lake Forrest. Peg Carry. Petting Party. Ginevra. Party"; November: "Ginevra and Margaret Cary to Yale game"; January, 1917:
"Final break with Ginevra"; June: "Ginevra engaged?"; September: "Oh Ginevra"; July, 1918: "Zelda. . . . Ginevra married."

When Scott Fitzgerald met her, Ginevra King was sixteen, a
junior at Westover, and already popular with the Ivy League boys.
Arthur Mizener has summed up their relationship: "For Ginevra,
he became for a time the most important of her many conquests.
As she said herself many years later, '. . . at this time I was defi-
nitely out for quantity not quality in beaux, and, although Scotty
was top man, I still wasn't serious enough not to want plenty of
other attention!' . . . To the end of his life he kept every letter
she ever wrote him (he had them typed up and bound; they run
to 227 pages). Born and brought up in the best circumstances in
Chicago and Lake Forest, Ginevra moved for him in a golden
haze." (*The Far Side of Paradise*, Boston, 1951, pp. 48-9) The
duration and depth of Fitzgerald's feelings toward the girl are
shown by a remark from a letter of November 9, 1938, to Frances
Turnbull: "In *This Side of Paradise* I wrote about a love affair
that was still bleeding as fresh as the skin wound on a haemophile."
(*The Letters of F. Scott Fitzgerald*, p. 578)

Between his infatuation with Kiddy Williams, Violet Stockton,
and other childhood sweethearts and his unrequited love for Ginevra King, he contributed two stories to the *Newman News*
which introduced the *femme fatale*. Though both heroes of these
stories are humiliated, neither is destroyed.

"A Luckless Santa Claus" begins: "Miss Harmon was responsible for the whole thing. If it had not been for her foolish whim,
Talbot would not have made a fool of himself, and—but I am
getting ahead of my story." What is "her foolish whim"? A challenge to wealthy, indolent, "faultlessly dressed" Harry Talbot to
give away twenty-five dollars, two dollars at a time, in an hour
and a half period one Christmas Eve, a challenge these words

explain: "Why you can't even spend money, much less earn it!" And how does her fiancé make "a fool of himself"? By accosting people who greet his generosity with a mistrust and contempt, which reach their climax when he gets badly mauled and must return "hatless, coatless, collarless, tieless." But Talbot is merely humiliated, not destroyed, for he soon deserts Miss Harmon for his maulers.

Technically, "The Trail of the Duke" closely resembles "A Luckless Santa Claus." We are given another aimless rich boy as victim and another silly girl friend as victimizer. Compared to Harry Talbot's experience, however, Dodson Garland's seems trivial since it hinges upon a simple misunderstanding instead of treating an ironic, thematically important circumstance. Mirabel Walmsley asks Dodson to find a missing duke. Thinking she means the Duke of Matterlane, he searches for him in the streets and in bars like Sherry's, Delmonico's, and Martin's, while he overimbibes ginger ale. When Dodson returns "crestfallen and broken-hearted," Mirabel, after revealing that the missing duke was a dog, invites him to meet the real duke the next day. He refuses and goes home, a reaction reminiscent of Harry Talbot's desertion of Miss Harmon.

The *femme fatale* plays a crucial role in four Princeton pieces published in 1917 by *The Nassau Literary Magazine* between January, the month Fitzgerald and Miss King made their final break, and October, the month before Fitzgerald was commissioned a second lieutenant in the regular army.

Both Isabelle of "Babes in the Woods" and Helen of "The Debutante" are based on Ginevra King. They differ from the girls who set the foolish quests, to the extent that calculation differs from capriciousness. Having played off another young man against him, Isabelle becomes Kenneth Powers' dinner partner. After achieving her purpose of attracting Kenneth's full attention, she abandons the first young man who has been "fascinated and totally unconscious that this was being done not for him but for the black eyes that glistened under the shining carefully watered hair a little to her left."

Although the young men in these stories are not destroyed, they suffer more than the humiliation to which their earlier counterparts were subjected. Throughout "The Debutante," a "huge pierglass" constantly reminds us of the narcissism of the heroine, the typical debutante soon to metamorphose into flapper or vamp. She coldly and clearly analyzes her fickleness and then heartlessly dismisses her most recent beau. Before he departs emotionally shattered, he has been brought to the verge of tears.

The most extreme instance of suffering at the hands of a woman occurs in "Sentiment—and the Use of Rouge," which deals with a slightly older set. In this story the hero's seduction by the *femme fatale* makes him a participant in the "new materialistic world" which he fears and despises. Through his actions he betrays not only the memory of his dead brother but also his own deepest convictions.

III

To one extent or another, the protagonists of *This Side of Paradise* (New York, 1920), *The Beautiful and Damned* (New York, 1922), *Tender Is the Night*, and *The Last Tycoon* combine a particular flaw *of* with general superiority *to* their society. Invariably, the flaw involves the *femme fatale*. Amory Blaine, though scarred, manages to survive three women, while Anthony Patch succumbs to one. Dick Diver is destroyed by his wife and Monroe Stahr sinks into a state of "emotional bankruptcy" partly because of the dead Minna.

The protagonists of *This Side of Paradise* and *The Beautiful and Damned* begin life with every advantage, the first being the son of wealthy, cultured midwesterners, and the second the grandson of a multimillionaire. Yet Amory loses his money, goes overseas, and must work in an advertising agency, and Anthony becomes insane after he has inherited his grandfather's fortune.

The protagonists of *Tender Is the Night* and *The Last Tycoon* fare no better. Dick degenerates from the serious, brilliant professional, whose learned articles have been standard in their line, to a "quack," a "shell." Monroe experiences Dick's same "lesion of vitality," but he perishes physically as well as deteriorating morally.

The points of similarity between the apprentice and mature fiction are scattered rather than clustered; no one juvenile work shares themes, characters, and techniques with any single work written during maturity. The only exception to this rule happens to be Fitzgerald's final college story, "The Pierian Springs and the Last Straw." It is also his best early story, despite the curious fact that he never placed it in *The Smart Set*, H. L. Mencken's chic *avant-garde* monthly, in which four of Fitzgerald's other college pieces were published. Perhaps Mencken never saw "The Pierian Springs" because Fitzgerald deliberately set the story aside, planning eventually to rework it. Whether that in fact happened cannot be determined, but, though qualitatively worlds apart, "The Pierian Springs" and *The Great Gatsby* bear so many and such striking similarities that the undergraduate story seems a kind of crude template for the masterwork that Fitzgerald was to publish seven and a half years later.

There are a number of resemblances between the story's protagonist, Uncle George, and the novel's antagonist, Tom Buchanan: both drink heavily, act promiscuously, and injure a finger of the woman they love. More crucial, however, are the resemblances between Uncle George and Jay Gatsby, Fitzgerald's best known male victim. About thirty years old and purveyors of disreputable merchandise, each assumes mythical stature. Gatsby is variously represented as Trimalchio and as a relative of Kaiser Wilhelm or Von Hindenburg, a German spy or a murderer. The nephew refers to his Uncle George as Romeo, Byron, Don Juan, Bernard Shaw, Havelock Ellis, "the Thomas Hardy of America," "the Balzac of his century." Jay Gatsby's personality is "an unbroken series of successful gestures" and Uncle George's is "a series of perfectly artificial mental tricks, . . . gestures." Jay Gatsby tells his story to Nick Carraway and Uncle George tells his to the nephew. Like Gatsby, who "took Daisy one still October night" and "felt married to her," George believes "life stopped at twenty-one one night in October at sixteen minutes after ten."

Like Gatsby, who "knew women early" and "became contemptuous of them," George becomes a misogynist. And like Gatsby, who also collected "presentable" trophies, George was inspired by a young lady "to do something for her, to get something to show her." Each is destroyed—Gatsby actually and George figuratively—because each allows abstract ideals to become incarnated in an unworthy woman and because each thinks he can repeat a past, which both story and novel frequently juxtapose to the present.

The resemblances between Myra Fulham of "The Pierian Springs" and Daisy Buchanan of *The Great Gatsby* are also remarkable. Uncle George applies adjectives to the former that apply equally well to the latter: "unprincipled," "selfish," "conceited," "uncontrolled." He claims, "When she wanted a boy there was no preliminary scouting among other girls for information, no sending out of tentative approaches meant to be retailed to him. There was the most direct attack by every faculty and gift that she possessed. She had no divergence of method—she just made you conscious to the highest degree that she was a girl." This sexuality expresses itself in Myra's "eternal mouth" and in Daisy's voice "full of money." Uncle George is betrayed first with a man "from another college" and then with "a crooked broker"—"the damn thief that robbed me of everything in this hellish world." Daisy betrays Gatsby with Tom.

The apprentice fiction of Scott Fitzgerald—stories composed between the ages of thirteen and twenty-one and submitted with unqualified success to school and college publications—discloses his amazing progress from the boy who wrote "The Mystery of the Raymond Mortgage" to the incipient artist who wrote "The Pierian Springs and the Last Straw." That the author's essential self emerges here is proved, among other evidence, by their containing his prototypal hero, the *homme manqué*, and heroine, the *femme fatale*.

The Mystery of the
Raymond Mortgage

The entry in Fitzgerald's "Ledger" for June, 1909, begins: "Wrote The Mystery of the Raymond Mortgage. Also 'Elavo' (or was that in Buffalo) and a complicated story of some knights." Actually, his literary apprenticeship had commenced two and a half years before. Another "Ledger" entry—this one for January, 1907—ends: "He began a history of the U.S. and also a detective story about a necklace that was hidden in a trapdoor under the carpet. Wrote celebrated essay on George Washington & St. Ignatius." Of all these pieces, only "The Mystery of the Raymond Mortgage," originally printed by the St. Paul Academy *Now and Then* (October, 1909) but reprinted fifty-one years later by *Ellery Queen's Mystery Magazine* (March, 1960), has survived.

Scott Fitzgerald once described the excitement of his fictional debut: "Never will I forget the Monday morning the numbers came out. The previous Saturday I had loitered desperately around the printers down-town and driven the man to indignation by persisting in trying to get a copy when the covers had not been bound on—finally, I had gone away and almost in tears. Nothing interested me until Monday, and when at recess, a big pile of the copies were brought in and delivered to the business manager I was so excited that I bounced in my seat and mumbled to myself, 'They're here! They're here!' until the whole school looked at me in amazement. I read my story through at least six times, and all that day I loitered in the corridors and counted the number of

men who were reading it, and tried to ask people casually, 'If they
had read it?' " (*Scott Fitzgerald*, pp. 28-9)

"The Mystery of the Raymond Mortgage" reflects the young
author's taste by unintentionally burlesquing the popular nine-
teenth-century detective story tradition running from Edgar Allan
Poe to Sir Arthur Conan Doyle, Maurice Leblanc, Gaston Leroux,
and Anna Katherine Green. The proper ingredients are there: a
missing document; a villainous servant; a stupid chief of police;
and a brilliant amateur investigator who, employing both deduc-
tive and inductive logic, solves the crime. There are even skillful
passages: exposition is conveyed through a newspaper account and
the opening introduces narrator, hero, and initial setting economi-
cally. Yet the story contains many of the faults to appear subse-
quently in the plays Fitzgerald wrote for the Elizabethan Dramatic
Club. "The Girl from the 'Lazy J'" (presented August, 1911),
The Captured Shadow (August 23, 1912), *Coward* (August 29
and September 2, 1913), and *Assorted Spirits* (September 8 and 9,
1914) also make use of "Whodunit" elements and complicated,
implausible, melodramatic plots. In the first, for example, when
his uncle enters kicking Tony Gonzoles, Jack Darcy muses, "Tony
—oh Tony! I wonder where that lazy greaser is?"

Absurdity runs rampant through "The Mystery of the Raymond
Mortgage." A valuable document has been stolen, but we never
learn by whom or why. Although the newspaper says, "Mayor
Proceeding to Scene of Crime," he never arrives, and although it
places the shots on Tuesday, John Syrel—who employs an agent
"in the shape of an Arab boy" named Smidy "for ten cents a day"—
places them on Friday. "The ablest detective in the force" allows
a total stranger to view Miss Raymond's body, which has been lying
about for days. His chief admits that he "might as well try to see
through a millstone as to try to fathom this mystery." He then lets
Syrel retain one of two death bullets, and until Syrel cautions him
to buy "a brace of revolvers," goes weaponless. How did Miss Raymond's head become "fearfully cut" and how did "a blood stain in

the shape of a hand" get on Mrs. Raymond's bed? What could Miss Raymond's lover have lifted from the ransacked bureau drawer? What was "a heavy Indian club" doing in Mrs. Raymond's room? And, finally, what train travels between Ithaca and Princeton?

The Mystery of the Raymond Mortgage

When I first saw John Syrel of the New York Daily News, he was standing before an open window of my house gazing out on the city. It was about six o'clock and the lights were just going on. All down Thirty-third street was a long line of gayly illuminated buildings. He was not a tall man, but thanks to the erectness of his posture, and the suppleness of his movement, it would take no athlete to tell that he was of fine build. He was twenty-three years old when I first saw him, and was already a reporter on the News. He was not a handsome man; his face was clean-shaven, and his chin showed him to be of strong character. His eyes and hair were brown.

As I entered the room he turned around slowly and addressed me in a slow, drawling tone: "I think I have the honor of speaking to Mr. Egan, chief of police." I assented, and he went on: "My name is John Syrel and my business,—to tell you frankly, is to learn all I can about that case of the Raymond mortgage.

I started to speak but he silenced me with a wave of his hand. "Though I belong to the staff of the Daily News," he continued, "I am not here as an agent of the paper." "I am not here," I interrupted coldly, "to tell every newspaper reporter or adventurer about private affairs. James, show this man out." Syrel turned without a word and I heard his steps echo up the driveway.

However, this was not destined to be the last time I ever saw Syrel, as events will show.

The morning after I first saw John Syrel, I proceeded to the scene of the crime to which he had alluded. On the train I picked up a newspaper and read the following account of the crime and theft, which had followed it:

"EXTRA"

"Great Crime Committeed in Suburbs of City"
"Mayor Proceeding to Scene of Crime"

"On the morning of July 1st, a crime and serious theft were committed on the outskirts of the city. Miss Raymond was killed and the body of a servant was found outside of the house. Mr. Raymond of Santuka Lake was awakened on Tuesday morning by a scream and two revolver shots which proceeded from his wife's room. He tried to open the door but it would not open. He was almost certain the door was locked from the inside, when suddenly it swung open disclosing a room in frightful disorder. On the center of the floor was a revolver and on his wife's bed was a blood stain in the shape of a hand. His wife was missing, but on a closer search he found his daughter under the bed, stone dead. The window was broken in two places. Miss Raymond had a bullet wound on her body and her head was fearfully cut. The body of a servant was found outside with a bullet hole through his head. Mrs. Raymond has not been found.

"The room was upset. The bureau drawers were out as if the murderer had been looking for something. Chief of Police Egan is on the scene of the crime, etc., etc."

Just then the conductor called out "Santuka!" The train came to a stop, and getting out of the car I walked up to the house. On the porch I met Gregson, who was supposed to be the ablest detective in the force. He gave me a plan of the house which he said he would like to have me look at before we went in.

"The body of the servant," he said, "is that of John Standish. He has been with the family twelve years and was a perfectly honest man. He was only thirty-two years old."

"The bullet which killed him was not found?" I asked.

"No," he answered; and then, "Well, you had better come in

and see for yourself. By the way, there was a fellow hanging
around here, who was trying to see the body. When I refused to
let him in, he went around to where the servant was shot and I
saw him go down on his knees on the grass and begin to search.
A few minutes later he stood up and leaned against a tree. Then
he came up to the house and asked to see the body again. I said
he could if he would go away afterwards. He assented, and when
he got inside the room he went down on his knees under the
bed and hunted around. Then he went over to the window and
examined the broken pane carefully. After that he declared himself satisfied and went down towards the hotel."

After I had examined the room to my satisfaction, I found that
I might as well try to see through a millstone as to try to fathom
this mystery. As I finished my investigation I met Gregson in the
laboratory.

"I suppose you heard about the mortgage," said he, as we went
down stairs. I answered in the negative, and he told me that a
valuable mortgage had disappeared from the room in which Miss
Raymond was killed. The night before Mr. Raymond had placed
the mortgage in a drawer and it had disappeared.

On my way to town that night I met Syrel again, and he bowed
cordially to me. I began to feel ashamed of myself for sending
him out of my house. As I went into the car the only vacant seat
was next to him. I sat down and apologized for my rudeness of
the day before. He took it lightly and, there being nothing to say,
we sat in silence. At last I ventured a remark.

"What do you think of the case?" "I don't think anything of
it as yet. I haven't had time yet."

Nothing daunted I began again. "Did you learn anything?"
Syrel dug his hand into his pocket and produced a bullet. I examined it.

"Where did you find it?" I asked.

"In the yard," he answered briefly.

At this I again relapsed into my seat. When we reached the
city, night was coming on. My first day's investigation was not
very successful.

My next day's investigation was no more successful than the first. My friend Syrel was not at home. The maid came into Mr. Raymond's room while I was there and gave notice that she was going to leave. "Mr. Raymond," she said, "there was queer noises outside my window last night. I'd like to stay, sir, but it grates on my nerves." Beyond this nothing happened, and I came home worn out. On the morning of the next day I was awakened by the maid who had a telegram in her hand. I opened it and found it was from Gregson. "Come at once," it said "startling development." I dressed hurriedly and took the first car to Santuka. When I reached the Santuka station, Gregson was waiting for me in a runabout. As soon as I got into the carriage Gregson told me what had happened.

"Some one was in the house last night. You know Mr. Raymond asked me to sleep there. Well, to continue, last night, about one, I began to be very thirsty. I went into the hall to get a drink from the faucet there, and as I was passing from my room (I sleep in Miss Raymond's room) into the hall I heard somebody in Mrs. Raymond's room. Wondering why Mr. Raymond was up at that time of night I went into the sitting room to investigate. I opened the door of Mrs. Raymond's room. The body of Miss Raymond was lying on the sofa. A man was kneeling beside it. His face was away from me, but I could tell by his figure that he was not Mr. Raymond. As I looked he got up softly and I saw him open a bureau drawer. He took something out and put it into his pocket. As he turned around he saw me, and I saw that he was a young man. With a cry of rage he sprang at me, and having no weapon I retreated. He snatched up a heavy Indian club and swung it over my head. I gave a cry which must have alarmed the house, for I knew nothing more till I saw Mr. Raymond bending over me."

"How did this man look," I asked. "Would you know him if you saw him again?" "I think not," he answered, "I only saw his profile."

"The only explanation I can give is this," said I. "The murderer was in Miss Raymond's room and when she came in he overpowered her and inflicted the gash. He then made for Mrs. Raymond's room and carried her off after having first shot Miss Raymond, who attempted to rise. Outside the house he met Standish, who attempted to stop him and was shot."

Gregson smiled. "That solution is impossible," he said.

As we reached the house I saw John Syrel, who beckoned me aside. "If you come with me," he said, "you will learn something that may be valuable to you." I excused myself to Gregson and followed Syrel. As we reached the walk he began to talk.

"Let us suppose that the murderer or murderess escaped from the house. Where would they go? Naturally they wanted to get away. Where did they go? Now, there are two railroad stations near by, Santuka and Lidgeville. I have ascertained that they did not go by Suntaka. So did Gregson. I supposed, therefore, that they went by Lidgeville. Gregson didn't; that's the difference. A straight line is the shortest distance between two points. I followed a straight line between here and Lidgeville. At first there was nothing. About two miles farther on I saw some footprints in a marshy hollow. They consisted of three footprints. I took an impression. Here it is. You see this one is a woman's. I have compared it with one of Mrs. Raymond's boots. They are identical. The others are mates. They belong to a man. I compared the bullet I found, where Standish was killed, with one of the remaining cartridges in the revolver that was found in Mrs. Raymond's room. They were mates. Only one shot had been fired and as I had found one bullet, I concluded that either Mrs. or Miss Raymond had fired the shot. I preferred to think Mrs. Raymond fired it because she had fled. Summing these things up and also taking into consideration that Mrs. Raymond must have had some cause to try to kill Standish, I concluded that John Standish killed Miss Raymond through the window of her mother's room, Friday night. I also conclude that Mrs. Raymond after ascertaining that her daughter was dead, shot Standish through the window and killed him. Horrified at what she had done she hid behind the door when Mr. Raymond came in. Then she ran down the back stairs. Going outside she stumbled upon the revolver Standish had used and picking it up took it with her. Somewhere between here and Lidgeville she met the owner of these footprints either by accident or design and walked with him to the station where they took the early train for Chicago. The station master did not see the man. He says that only a woman bought a ticket, so I concluded that the young man didn't go. Now you must tell me what Gregson told you."

"How did you know all this," exclaimed I astonished. And then I told him about the midnight visitor. He did not appear to be much astonished, and he said "I guess that the young man is our friend of the footprints. Now you had better go get a brace of revolvers and pack your suit case if you wish to go with me to find this young man and Mrs. Raymond, whom I think is with him."

Greatly surprised at what I had heard I took the first train back to town. I bought a pair of fine Colt revolvers, a dark lantern, and two changes of clothing. We went over to Lidgeville and found that a young man had left on the six o'clock train for Ithaca. On reaching Ithaca we found that he had changed trains and was now half way to Princeton, New Jersey. It was five o'clock, but we took a fast train and expected to overtake him half way between Ithaca and Princeton. What was our chagrin when on reaching the slow train, to find he had gotten off at Indianous and was now probably safe. Thoroughly disappointed we took the train for Indianous. The ticket seller said that a young man in a light gray suit had taken a bus to the Raswell Hotel. We found the bus which the station master said he had taken, in the street. We went up to the driver and he admitted that he had started for the Raswell Hotel in his cab.

"But," said the old fellow, "when I reached there, the fellow had clean disappeared, an' I never got his fare."

Syrel groaned; it was plain that we had lost the young man. We took the next train for New York and telegraphed to Mr. Raymond that we would be down Monday. Sunday night, however, I was called to the phone and recognized Syrel's voice. He directed me to come at once to five hundred thirty-four Chestnut street. I met him on the doorstep.

"What have you heard?" I asked. "I have an agent in Indianous," he replied, "in the shape of an Arab boy whom I employ for ten cents a day. I told him to spot the woman and today I got a telegram from him (I left him money to send one), saying to come at once. So come on." We took the train for Indianous. "Smidy," the young Arab, met us at the station.

"You see, sur, it's dis way. You says, 'Spot de guy wid dat hack,' and I says I would. Dat night a young dude comes out of er house on Pine street and gives the cabman a ten-dollar bill. An den he went back into the house and a minute after he comes out wid a woman, an' den day went down here a little way an' goes into a house farther down the street, I'll show you de place."

We followed Smidy down the street until we arrived at a corner house. The groundfloor was occupied by a cigar store, but the second floor was evidently for rent. As we stood there a face appeared at the window and, seeing us, hastily retreated. Syrel pulled a picture from his pocket. "It's she," he exclaimed, and calling us to follow he dashed into a little side door. We heard voices upstairs, a shuffle of feet and a noise as if a door had been shut.

"Up the stairs," shouted Syrel, and we followed him, taking two steps at a bound. As we reached the top landing we were met by a young man.

"What right have you to enter this house?" he demanded.

"The right of the law," replied Syrel.

"I didn't do it" broke out the young man. "It was this way. Agnes Raymond loved me—she did not love Standish—he shot her; and God did not let her murder go unrevenged. It was well Mrs. Raymond killed him, for his blood would have been on my hands. I went back to see Agnes before she was buried. A man came in. I knocked him down. I didn't know until a moment ago that Mrs. Raymond had killed him

"I forgot Mrs. Raymond" screamed Syrel, "where is she?"

"She is out of your power forever," said the young man.

Syrel brushed past him and, with Smidy and I following, burst open the door of the room at the head of the stairs. We rushed in.

On the floor lay a woman, and as soon as I touched her heart I knew she was beyond the doctor's skill.

"She has taken poison," I said. Syrel looked around, the young man had gone. And we stood there aghast in the presence of death.

Reade, Substitute Right Half

Hardly more than a sketch, Scott Fitzgerald's second contribution to the *Now and Then* (February, 1910; reprinted in *The Princeton University Library Chronicle*, Autumn, 1955) succeeds precisely where "The Mystery of the Raymond Mortgage" failed: "Reade, Substitute Right Half" is not overplotted and so does not run the concomitant risks of melodrama and implausibility.

Fitzgerald was obsessed by football. A "Ledger" entry of September, 1905, ends, "He had a complete football outfit with shinguards," and thirty-five years later, on the day of his death (December 21, 1940), he was making notes for next year's team in a *Princeton Alumni Weekly*.

When Princeton accepted him, Fitzgerald wired home, "ADMITTED SEND FOOTBALL PADS AND SHOES IMMEDIATELY PLEASE WAIT TRUNK." That at 138 pounds he was not heavy enough for college football is referred to in the first of three famous "Crack-Up" articles published by *Esquire* during 1936: "As the twenties passed, with my own twenties marching a little ahead of them, my two juvenile regrets—at not being big enough (or good enough) to play football in college, and at not getting overseas during the war—resolved themselves into childish waking dreams of imaginary heroism."

At the Newman School he had experienced an even more humiliating *defeat* which he *admitted* even more candidly. In a game "up on the Hudson," Fitzgerald, having knocked down a pass instead of intercepting it, was unfairly accused of being "yellow." He commented in the self-revelatory "Author's House": "The point is it inspired me to write a poem for the school paper which made me as big a hit with my father as if I had become

a football hero. So when I went home that Christmas vacation
it was in my mind that if you weren't able to function in action
you might at least be able to tell about it, because you felt the
same intensity—it was a back door way out of facing reality."
"Football" was printed on p. 19 of a 1911 *Newman News* the
year after he had published an article about sports heroes, "S.P.A.
Men in College Athletics," in the *Now and Then:*

> Now they're ready, now they're waiting,
> Now he's going to place the ball.
> There, you hear the referee's whistle,
> As of old the baton's fall.
> See him crouching. Yes, he's got it;
> Now he's off around the end.
> Will the interference save him?
> Will the charging line now bend?
> Good, he's free; no, see that halfback
> Gaining up behind him slow.
> Crash! they're down; he threw him nicely,—
> Classy tackle, hard and low.
> Watch that line, now crouching waiting,
> In their jersies white and black;
> Now they're off and charging, making
> Passage for the plunging back.
> Buck your fiercest, run your fastest,
> Let the straight arm do the rest.
> Oh, they got him; never mind, though,
> He could only do his best.
> What is this? A new formation.
> Look! their end acts like an ass.
> See, he's beckoning for assistance,
> Maybe it's a forward pass.
> Yes, the ball is shot to fullback,
> He, as calmly as you please,
> Gets it, throws it to the end; he
> Pulls the pigskin down with ease.

Now they've got him. No, they haven't.
See him straight-arm all those fools.
Look, he's clear. Oh, gee! don't stumble.
Faster, faster, for the school.
There's the goal, now right before you,
Ten yards, five yards, bless your name!
Oh! you Newman, 1911,
You know how to play the game.

Throughout his school days and throughout his life, football remained to Scott Fitzgerald a symbol of the unattainable—"the most intense and dramatic spectacle since the Olympic games" ("Princeton," *College Humor*, December, 1927)—and the football player merged with that of the gallant soldier, decorated with medals, into his concept of the modern hero. To the man who felt himself unsuccessful at both, football and war became what bullfighting was to Hemingway—the last opportunity in an unheroic age for man to act heroically.

Andrew Turnbull has described Fitzgerald's football experiences during the "Reade" period: "Once, in a football game, he lay on the field after a scrimmage with the breath apparently knocked out of him. A moment later he was up, eager to resume play, but the coach made him quit because his chest was hurting (it was later found that he had a broken rib). As he limped off the field, he said, 'Well, boys, I've given my all—now let's see what you can do.' Another time he dropped a pass that lost the game and . . . burst into tears. . . . Perhaps his most memorable feat was performed against a much heavier team from Central High. . . . But again he was hurt and had to leave the game. A friend who called on him next day found him strapped up and lying in bed, clearly relishing the role of the wounded veteran." (*Scott Fitzgerald*, p. 21)

The vitality of "Reade, Substitute Right Half," whose central figure is the author's first triumphant underdog, may very well stem from the emotional force of wish-fulfillment.

Reade, Substitute Right Half

"Hold! Hold! Hold!" The slogan thundered up the field to where the battered, crimson warriors trotted wearily into their places again. The blues attack this time came straight at center and was good for a gain of seven yards. "Second down, three," yelled the referee, and again the attack came straight at center. This time there was no withstanding the rush and the huge Hilton fullback crushed through the crimson line again and shaking off his many tacklers, staggered on toward the Warrentown goal.

The midget Warrentown quarter-back ran nimbly up the field and, dodging the interference, shot in straight at the fullback's knees throwing him to the ground. The teams sprang back into line again, but Hearst, the crimson right tackle, lay still upon the ground. The right half was shifted to tackle and Berl, the captain, trotted over to the sidelines to ask the advice of the coaches.

"Who have we got for half, sir?" he inquired of the hear coach.

"Suppose you try Reade," answered the coach, and calling to one of the figures on the pile of straw, which served as a seat for the substitutes, he beckoned to him. Pulling off his sweater, a light haired stripling trotted over to the coach.

"Pretty light," said Berl as he surveyed the form before him.

"I guess that's all we have, though," answered the coach. Reade was plainly nervous as he shifted his weight from one foot to the other and fidgeted with the end of his jersey.

"Oh, I guess he'll do," said Berl. "Come on kid," and they trotted off on the field.

The teams quickly lined up and the Hilton quarter gave the signal "6-8-7G." The play came between guard and tackle, but

31

before the full-back could get started a lithe form shot out from
the Warrentown line and brought him heavily to the ground.
"Good work, Reade," said Berl, as Reade trotted back into his
place, and blushing at the compliment he crouched low in the
line and waited for the play. The center snapped the ball to quarter, who, turning, was about to give it to the half. The ball slipped
from his grasp and he reached for it, but too late. Reade had
slipped in between the end and tackle and dropped on the ball.
"Good one, Reade," shouted Mridle, the Warrentown quarter,
as he came racing up, crying signals as he ran. Signal "48—10G—
37," It was Reade around left end, but the pass was bad and the
quarter dropped the ball. Reade scooped it up on a run and
raced around left end. In the delay which had been caused by the
fumble Reade's interference had been broken up and he must
shift for himself even as he rounded the end he was thrown with
a thud by the blue full-back. He had gained but a yard. "Never
mind, Reade," said the quarter, "my fault." The ball was snapped,
but again the pass was bad and a Hilton line man fell on the
ball.

Then began a steady march up the field toward the Warrentown
goal. Time and time again Reade slipped through the Hilton line
and nailed the runner before he could get started. But slowly Hilton pushed down the field toward the Warrentown goal. When the
Blues were on the Crimson's ten-yard line their quarter-back made
his only error of judgment during the game. He gave the signal
for a forward pass. The ball was shot to the full-back, who turned
to throw it to the right half. As the pigskin left his hand, Reade
leaped upward and caught the ball. He stumbled for a moment,
but, soon getting his balance, started out for the Hilton goal with
a long string of Crimson and Blue men spread out behind
him. He had a start of about five yards on his nearest opponent,
but this distance was decreased to three before he had passed his
own forty-five-yard line. He turned his head and looked back. His
pursuer was breathing heavily and Reade saw what was coming.
He was going to try a diving tackle. As the man's body shot out

straight for him he stepped out of the way and the man fell harm-
lessly past him, missing him by a foot.

From there to the goal line it was easy running, and as Reade
laid the pigskin on the ground and rolled happily over beside it
he could just hear another slogan echo down the field: "One
point—two points—three points—four points—five points. Reade!
Reade! Reade!"

A Debt of Honor

and

The Room With the Green Blinds

Both these stories may have their inspiration in Civil War anecdotes. A January, 1902, "Ledger" entry reads, "He remembers Jack Butler who had two or three facinating books about the Civil War." But a more likely source is Edward Fitzgerald, Scott's father, whose affinities with the conflict Andrew Turnbull has recorded: "When Edward Fitzgerald was nine, he had rowed Confederate spies across the river, and all one morning he sat on a fence watching Early's battalions stream toward Washington in the last Confederate thrust. The Civil War was the drama of his youth and indeed of his entire life." (*Scott Fitzgerald*, p. 6)

The protagonist of Fitzgerald's Civil War play, *Coward*, discovers that war, like football, can provide an opportunity to act heroically. For the mature fiction, it would also provide historical awareness and perspective. The "Ledger" is full of early references to the American Revolution and the Civil War, one of January, 1903, stating, "He begins to remember many things . . . a history of the United States which father brought me; he became a child of the American Revolution." And the author's library at Princeton suggests that he read more books in the field of history (including military strategy) than in any other field except literature.

Of all wars, the American Civil War exercised the most profound influence on him. Edward Fitzgerald had been descended from the Scotts and Keys, Maryland families which had served colonial legislatures and produced Francis Scott Key, whom Fitzgerald thought of as a great, great uncle. Given his tendency to identify autobiographical and historical events (he once compared personal happiness and despair to the country's Boom and Depression), it is probable that his financially inept but "old American stock" father came to symbolize pre-Civil War southern aristocracy while his mother's financially successful but "black Irish" relatives came to represent post-Civil War northern *nouveaux riches*. At any rate, the fathers of Nick Carraway and Dick Diver act as moral touchstones in books whose heroes are destroyed by the new materialistic society. Scott Fitzgerald, who attended the southerner's northern university and married a southern belle, would define the Civil War as the "broken link in the continuity of American life." ("Princeton")

"A Debt of Honor" appeared in the March, 1910, issue of *Now and Then* and "The Room With the Green Blinds" in the June, 1911, issue.

A Debt of Honor

"Prayle!"

"Here."

"Martin!"

"Absent."

"Sanderson!"

"Here."

"Carlton, for sentry duty!"

"Sick."

"Any volunteers to take his place?"

"Me, me," said Jack Sanderson, eagerly.

"All right," said the captain and went on with the roll.

It was a very cold night. Jack never quite knew how it came about. He had been wounded in the hand the day before and his gray jacket was stained a bright red where he had been hit by a stray ball. And "number six" was such a long post. From way up by the general's tent to way down by the lake. He could feel a faintness stealing over him. He was very tired and it was getting very dark—very dark.

They found him there, sound alseep, in the morning worn out by the fatigue of the march and the fight which had followed it. There was nothing the matter with him save the wounds, which were slight, and military rules were very strict. To the last day of his life Jack always remembered the sorrow in his captain's voice as he read aloud the dismal order.

Camp Bowling Green, C. S. A. Jan. 15, 1863, U. S.

For falling asleep while in a position of trust at a sentry post, private John Sanderson is hereby condemned to be shot at sunrise on Jan, 16, 1863.

By order of
ROBERT E. LEE,
Lieutenant General Commanding.

Jack never forgot the dismal night and the march which followed it. They tied a hankerchief over his head and led him a little apart to a wall which bounded one side of the camp. Never had life seemed so sweet.

General Lee in his tent thought long and seriously upon the matter.

"He is so awfully young and of good family too; but camp discipline must be enforced. Still it was not much of an offense for such a punishment. The lad was over tired and wounded. By George, he shall go free if I risk my reputation. Sergeant, order private John Sanderson to be brought before me."

"Very well, sir," and saluting, the orderly left the tent.

Jack was brought in, supported by two soldiers, for a reaction had set in after his narrow escape from death.

"Sir," said General Lee sternly, "on account of your extreme youth you will get off with a reprimand but see that it never happens again, for, if it should, I shall not be so lenient."

"General," answered Jack drawing himself up to his full height, "The Conferderate States of America shall never have cause to regret that I was not shot;" and Jack was led away, still trembling, but happy in the knowledge of a new found life.

Six weeks after with Lee's army near Chancellorsville. The success of Fredricksburg had made possible this advance of the Confederate arms. The firing had just commenced when a courier rode up to General Jackson.

"Colonel Barrows says sir, that the enemy have possession of a small frame house on the outskirts of the woods and it overlooks our earthworks. Has he your permission to take it by assault?"

"My compliments to Colonel Barrows and say that I cannot spare more than twenty men but that he is welcome to charge with that number," answered the General.

"Yes, sir," and the orderly setting spurs to his horse rode away.

Five minutes later a column of men from the 3rd Virginia burst out from the woods and ran toward the house. A galling fire broke out from the Federal lines and many a brave man fell, among whom was their leader, a young lieutenant. Jack Sanderson sprang to the front and waving his gun encouraged the men onward. Half way between the Confederate lines and the house was a small mound, and behind this the men threw themselves to get a minute's respite.

A minute later a figure sprang up and ran toward the house, and before the Union troops saw him he was half way across the bullet swept clearing. Then the federal fire was directed at him. He staggered for a moment and placed his hand to his forehead. On he ran and reaching the house he quickly opened the door and went inside. A minute later a pillar of flame shot out of the windows of the house and almost immediately afterwards the Federal occupants were in full flight. A long cheer rolled along the Confederate lines and then the word was given to charge and they charged sweeping all before them. That night the searchers wended their way to the half burned house. There on the floor, beside the mattress he had set on fire, lay the body of him who had once been John Sanderson, private, third Virginia. He had paid his debt.

The Room With the Green Blinds

I

It was ominous looking enough in broad daylight, with its dull, brown walls, and musty windows. The garden, if it might be called so, was simply a mass of overgrown weeds, and the walk was falling to pieces, the bricks crumbling from the touch of time. Inside it was no better. Rickety old three-legged chairs covered with a substance that had once been plush, were not exactly hospitable looking objects. And yet this house was part of the legacy my grandfather had left me. In his will had been this clause: "The house, as it now stands, and all that is inside it, shall go to my grandson, Robert Calvin Raymond, on his coming to the age of twenty-one years. I furthermore desire that he shall not open the room at the end of the corridor, on the second floor until Carmatle falls. He may fix up three rooms of the house as modern as he wishes, but let the others remain unchanged. He may keep but one servant."

To a poor young man with no outlook in life, and no money, but a paltry eight hundred a year, this seemed a windfall when counted with the twenty-five thousand dollars that went with it. I resolved to fix up my new home, and so started South to Macon, Ga., near which my grandfather's house was situated. All the evening on the Pullman I had thought about that clause, "He shall not open the room at the end of the corridor on the second floor until Carmatle falls." Who was Carmatle? And what did it mean when it said, "When Carmatle falls?" In vain I supposed and guessed and thought; I could make no sense of it.

When I finally arrived at the house, I lighted one of a box of candles which I had brought with me and walked up the creaking stairs to the third floor and down a long, narrow corridor covered with cobwebs and bugs of all sorts till I finally came to a massive oaken door which barred my further progress. On the door I could just make out with the aid of the candle the initials J. W. B. in red paint. The door was barred on the outside by heavy iron bars, effectually barricaded against anybody entering or going out. Suddenly, without even a warning flicker my candle went out, and I found myself in complete darkness. Though I am not troubled with weak nerves, I confess I was somewhat startled by this, for there was not a breath of air stirring. I relit the candle and walked out of the corridor down to the room of the three-legged chairs. As it was now almost nine o'clock and as I was tired after my day of traveling, I soon fell off to sleep.

How long I slept I do not know. I awoke suddenly and sat bolt upright on the lounge. For far down the downstairs hall I heard approaching footsteps, and a second later saw the reflection of a candle on the wall outside my door. I made no noise but as the steps came closer I crept softly to my feet. Another sound and the intruder was directly outside and I had a look at him. The flickering flame of the candle shone on a strong, handsome face, fine brown eyes and a determined chin. A stained grey Confederate uniform covered a magnificent form and here and there a blood stain made him more weird as he stood looking straight ahead with a glazed stare. His clean shaven face seemed strangely familiar to me, and some instinct made me connect him with the closed door on the right wing.

I came to myself with a start and crouched to leap at him, but some noise I made must have alarmed him, for the candle was suddenly extinguished and I brought up against a chair, nursing a bruised shin. I spent the rest of the night trying to connect the clause in my uncle's will with this midnight prowler.

When morning came, things began to look clearer, and I resolved to find out whether I had been dreaming or whether I had had a Confederate officer for a guest. I went into the hall and searched for any sign which might lead to a revelation of the mystery. Sure enough, just outside my door was a tallow stain. About ten yards further on was another, and I found myself following a trail of spots along the hall, and upstairs toward the left wing of the house. About twenty feet from the door of the forbidden room they stopped; neither was there any trace of anyone having gone further. I walked up to the door and tried it to make sure that no one could possibly go in or out. Then I descended and, sauntering out, went around to the east wing to see how it looked from the outside. The room had three windows, each of which was covered with a green blind, and with three iron bars. To make sure of this I went around to the barn, a tumbly old structure, and, by dint of much exertion, succeeded in extracting a ladder from a heap of debris behind it. I placed this against the house, and climbing up, tested each bar carefully. There was no deception. They were firmly set in the concrete sill.

Therefore, there could be but one explanation, the man concealed there must have a third way of getting out, some sort of secret passageway. With this thought in mind I searched the house from garret to cellar, but not a sign could I see of any secret entrance. Then I sat down to think it over.

In the first place there was somebody concealed in the room in the east wing. I had no doubt of that, who was in the habit of making midnight visits to the front hall. Who was Carmatle? It was an unusual name, and I felt if I could find its posesssor I could unravel this affair.

Aha! now I had it. Carmatle, the governor of Georgia; why had I not thought of that before? I resolved that that afternoon I would start for Atlanta to see him.

II.

"Mr. Carmattyle, I believe?"

"At your service."

"Governor, it's rather a personal matter I have come to see you about and I may have made a mistake in identity. Do you know anything about 'J. W. B.' or did you ever know a man with those initials?"

The governor paled.

"Young man, tell me where you heard those initials and what brought you here?"

In as few words as possible I related to him my story, beginning with the will and ending with my theories regarding it.

When I had finished, the governor rose to his feet.

"I see it all; I see it all. Now with your permission I shall spend a night with you in your house in company with a friend of mine who is in the secret service. If I am right, concealed in that house is—well," he broke off. "I had better not say now, for it may be only a remarkable coincidence. Meet me at the station in half an hour, and you had better bring a revolver.

Six o'clock found us at the manor and the governor and I with the detective he had brought along, a fellow by the name of Butler, proceeded at once to the room.

After half an hour's labor we succeeded in finding no such thing as a passageway, secret or otherwise. Being tired I sat down to rest and in doing so my hand touched a ledge projecting from the wall. Instantly a portion of the wall swung open, disclosing an opening about three feet square. Instantly the governor, with the agility of a cat, was through it and his form disappeared from view. We grasped the situation and followed him. I found myself crawling along on hard stone in black darkness. Suddenly a shot resounded, and another. Then the passageway came to an end. We were in a room magnificently hung with oriental draperies, the walls covered with medieval armor and ancient swords, shields and battle axes. A red lamp on the table threw a lurid glare over all and cast a red glow on a body which lay at the foot of a Turkish divan. It was the Confederate officer, shot through the heart, for the life blood was fast staining his grey uniform red. The governor was standing near the body, a smoking revolver in his hand.

"Gentlemen," said he, "Let me present to you John Wilkes Booth, the slayer of Albraham Lincoln."

III.

Mr. Carmatle, you will explain this I hope."

"Certainly," and drawing up a chair the governor began:

"My son and I served in Forest's cavalry during the Civil War, and being on a scouting expedition did not hear of Lee's surrender at Appomatox until about three months afterwards. As we were riding southward along the Cumberland pike we met a man riding down the road. Having struck up an acquaintance, as travelers do, we camped together, the next morning the man was gone, together with my son's old horse and my son's old uniform, leaving his new horse and new civilian suit instead. We did not know what to make of this, but never suspected who this man was. My son and I separated and I never saw him again. He was bound for his aunt's in Western Maryland and one morning he was shot by some Union soldiers in a barn where he had tried to snatch a minute's rest on the way. The story was given out to the public that it was Booth that was shot but I knew and the government knew that my innocent son had been shot by mistake and that John Wilkes Booth, the man who had taken his horse and clothes had escaped. For four years I hunted Booth, but until I heard you mention the initials J. W. B. I had heard no word of him. As it was, when I found him he shot first. I think that his visit to the hall in the Confederate uniform was simply to frighten you away. The fact that your grandfather was a Southern sympathizer probably had protected him all these years. So now, gentlemen, you have heard my story. It rests with you whether this gets no farther than us three here and the government, or whether I shall be proclaimed a murderer and brought to trial."

"You are as innocent as Booth is guilty," said I. "My lips shall be forever sealed."

And we both pressed forward and took him by the hand.

A Luckless Santa Claus,
The Trail of the Duke
and
Pain and the Scientist

At the Newman School, where Scott Fitzgerald spent most of his fifteenth and sixteenth years, he published three stories in addition to serving on the *News'* editorial staff. None of these is similar to any of the *Now and Then* pieces. And while one, "Pain and the Scientist" (1913), resembles the other two technically, it otherwise stands alone among the Newman pieces. All three employ the O. Henry surprise ending, but only "A Luckless Santa Claus" (Christmas, 1912) and "The Trail of the Duke" (1913) introduce the *femme fatale* and treat the wealthy class in an urban setting. "Pain and the Scientist" is a far more boyish story, a farce-satire attacking Christian Science. Its protagonist, a man of modest means, moves from some unspecified location to a fictitious place called Middleton.

New York City had been the opening, though not the central setting, of "The Mystery of the Raymond Mortgage." Except for the first few sentences—". . . It was about six o'clock and the lights were just going on. All down Thirty-third street was a long line of gayly illuminated buildings."—references to the metropolis in the 1909 story are quite perfunctory. Not so with "A Luckless Santa Claus" and "The Trail of the Duke." The heroine of the

44

first story lives "somewhere east of Broadway" and the hero of the second owns a "house on upper Fifth Avenue." Largely because of Harry Talbot's walk down Broadway to Union Square, Cooper Square, the Bowery, then up Third Avenue, place takes on greater significance and utility in "A Luckless Santa Claus" than in "The Trail of the Duke." This seems particularly unfortunate considering that the initial paragraph of the latter represents Fitzgerald's most ambitious descriptive passage to date. New York would appear four times throughout the apprentice fiction; southern locations three times; Princeton and London twice.

One of the Basil Duke Lee stories, "Forging Ahead," has expressed the midwestern boy's thrill over departing for boarding school in the East: "Beyond the dreary railroad stations of Chicago and the night fires of Pittsburgh, back in the old states, something went on that made his heart beat fast with excitement. He was attuned to the vast, breathless bustle of New York, to the metropolitan days and nights that were tense as singing wires. Nothing needed to be imagined there, for it was all the very stuff of romance—life was as vivid and satisfactory as in books and dreams." (Arthur Mizener [ed.], *Afternoon of an Author*, Princeton, 1957, p. 34) And once in the East, Fitzgerald's "Ledger" records: "Trips to New York" (January, 1912); "More New York trips" (April, 1912); "Shows in New York" (November, 1912). These shows included *The Little Millionaire*, with George M. Cohan, *The Quaker Girl*, with Ina Claire, *Over the River*, and *The Private Secretary*. Since they inspired him to start writing librettos which would lead to his work on three Princeton Triangle Club productions (*Fie! Fie! Fi-Fi!* of 1914-1915, *The Evil Eye* of 1915-1916 and *Safety First* of 1916-1917), New York supplied more than just a setting for his apprentice fiction.

Money had been a minor factor in two stories prior to "A Luckless Santa Claus" and "The Trail of the Duke." The family of "The Mystery of the Raymond Mortgage" had employed servants and the protagonist of "The Room with the Green Blinds" had inherited a house and twenty-five thousand dollars—all this supplemented by the idea of "mortgage" in the first and of "legacy" in the second. But neither had treated the indolent rich, who now make their initial appearance. Harry Talbot of "A Luckless Santa Claus" spends his time playing golf and running up "some very choice bills" with his father's money. Dodson Garland of "The Trail of the Duke" "lay on a divan in the billiard room and consumed oceans of mint juleps, as he grumbled at the polo that had kept him in town, the cigarettes, the butler, and occasionally breaking the Second Commandment." These two do not represent the typical hero of the early stories, for he is a middle-class boy who has yet to suffer on specifically economic grounds.

The mature Scott Fitzgerald's American "aristocrat by wealth" may be recognized by a certain nobility of bearing which is the product of what the Renaissance would have termed "grace," the ability to be at ease in all situations. The true aristocrat was a "thoroughbred," whether young or old, a condition produced by training and education: as children the rich are taught to speak well, "their words and sentences were all crisp and clear and not run together as ours are." ("The Rich Boy," *All the Sad Young Men*, p. 2) But more important is the confidence of established money and social position.

Although a lower- or middle-class boy may develop certain aristocratic qualities, he will not be able to acquire the same degree of "grace" that the rich have. It is conceivable, however, that his children, like Dick Humbird (*This Side of Paradise*), son of a newly rich father, will someday grow up with the confidence of an Anson Hunter, "the rich boy," who was born into solid wealth. This same confidence enables the rich to greet each other with cheerful familiarity and to dress in an informal but correct way.

Wealth and aristocracy were not always synonymous in Scott Fitzgerald's mind. Sometimes he admired and envied the leisure class (as he did athletes and soldiers) and sometimes he despised it. Although wealth may lead to the aristocratic qualities of courage, honor, and intelligence, too often the rich exemplify opposite qualities; they can be cliquish, undependable, corrupt, selfish, fickle, idle, shiftless, unaware, self-indulgent, and cynical.

The author's feelings toward the poor would show no such

ambivalence. To him, they were stupid and slavish. Yet, he once said that if he were unable to live with the rich, his next choice would be the poor. Anything was better than the unstable middle class.

Like many of his contemporaries, Fitzgerald pointed out the moral and cultural limitations of his own social strata, though his was usually not a diatribe against the bourgeoisie like those of Sinclair Lewis or H. L. Mencken. Fitzgerald's contribution to the study of the American middle class would lie in another direction.

If the instability of this group often made it appear ridiculous, that very instability also rendered it pathetic and tragic. Because the middle class had just enough income to allow it partial mobility, its economic position tended to reinforce among the more imaginative the typically American notion that one need only strive for a goal to achieve it. But because the middle class was not wealthy enough to be completely mobile, these goals and ideals were seldom realized. Scott Fitzgerald's bourgeois heroes believe that anything is possible and so become disillusioned in the end. He would not write the tragedy of the rich, nor of the poor. He would write the tragedy of the unstable middle class.

A Luckless Santa Claus

Miss Harmon was responsible for the whole thing. If it had not been for her foolish whim, Talbot would not have made a fool of himself, and—but I am getting ahead of my story.

It was Christmas Eve. Salvation Army Santa Clauses with highly colored noses proclaimed it as they beat upon rickety paper chimneys with tin spoons. Package laden old bachelors forgot to worry about how many slippers and dressing gowns they would have to thank people for next day, and joined in the general air of excitement that pervaded busy Manhattan.

In the parlor of a house situated on a dimly lighted residence street somewhere east of Broadway, sat the lady who, as I have said before, started the whole business. She was holding a conversation half frivolous, half sentimental, with a faultlessly dressed young man who sat with her on the sofa. All of this was quite right and proper, however, for they were engaged to be married in June.

"Harry Talbot," said Dorothy Harmon, as she rose and stood laughing at the merry young gentleman beside her, "if you aren't the most ridiculous boy I ever met, I'll eat that terrible box of candy you brought me last week!"

"Dorothy," reproved the young man, "you should receive gifts in the spirit in which they are given. That box of candy cost me much of my hard earned money."

"Your hard earned money, indeed!" scoffed Dorothy. "You know very well that you never earned a cent in your life. Golf and dancing—that is the sum total of your occupations. Why, you can't even spend money, much less earn it!"

"My dear Dorothy, I succeeded in running up some very choice bills last month, as you will find if you consult my father."

"That's not spending your money. That's wasting it. Why, I don't think you could give away twenty-five dollars in the right way to save your life."

"But why on earth," remonstrated Harry, "should I want to give away twenty-five dollars?"

"Because," explained Dorothy, "that would be real charity. It's nothing to charge a desk to your father and have it sent to me, but to give money to people you don't know is something."

"Why, any old fellow can give away money," protested Harry.

"Then," exclaimed Dorothy, "we'll see if you can. I don't believe that you could give twenty-five dollars in the course of an evening if you tried."

"Indeed, I could."

"Then try it!" And Dorothy, dashing into the hall, took down his coat and hat and placed them in his reluctant hands. "It is now half-past eight. You be here by ten o'clock."

"But, but," gasped Harry.

Dorothy was edging him towards the door.

"How much money have you?" she demanded.

Harry gloomily put his hand in his pocket and counted out a handful of bills.

"Exactly twenty-five dollars and five cents."

"Very well! Now listen! These are the conditions. You go out and give this money to anybody you care to whom you have never seen before. Don't give more than two dollars to any one person. And be back here by ten o'clock with no more than five cents in your pocket."

"But," declared Harry, still backing towards the door, "I *want* my twenty-five dollars."

"Harry," said Dorothy sweetly, "I am *surprised!*" and with that, she slammed the door in his face.

"I insist," muttered Harry, "that this is a most unusual proceeding."

He walked down the steps and hesitated.

"Now," he thought, "Where shall I go?"

He considered a moment and finally started off towards Broadway. He had gone about half a block when he saw a gentleman in a top hat approaching. Harry hesitated. Then he made up his mind, and, stepping towards the man, emitted what he intended for a pleasant laugh but what sounded more like a gurgle, and loudly vociferated, "Merry Christmas, friend!"

"The same to you," answered he of the top hat, and would have passed on, but Harry was not to be denied.

"My good fellow"—He cleared his throat. "Would you like me to give you a little money?"

"What?" yelled the man.

"You might need some money, don't you know, to—er—buy the children—a—a rag doll," he finished brilliantly.

The next moment his hat went sailing into the gutter, and when he picked it up the man was far away.

"There's five minutes wasted," muttered Harry, as, full of wrath towards Dorothy, he strode along his way. He decided to try a different method with the next people he met. He would express himself more politely.

A couple approached him,—a young lady and her escort. Harry halted directly in their path and, taking off his hat, addressed them.

"As it is Christmas, you know, and everybody gives away—er—articles, why"—

"Give him a dollar, Billy, and let's go on," said the young lady.

Billy obediently thrust a dollar into Harry's hand, and at that moment the girl gave a cry of surprise.

"Why, it's Harry Talbot," she exclaimed, "begging!"

But Harry heard no more. When he realized that he knew the girl he turned and sped like an arrow up the street, cursing has foolhardiness in taking up the affair at all.

He reached Broadway and started slowly down the gaily lighted thoroughfare, intending to give money to the street Arabs he met. All around him was the bustle of preparation. Everywhere swarmed people happy in the pleasant concert of their own generosity. Harry felt strangely out of place as he wandered aimlessly along. He was used to being catered to and bowed before, but here no one spoke to him, and one or two even had the audacity to smile at him and wish him a "Merry Christmas." He nervously accosted a passing boy.

"I say, little boy, I'm going to give you some money."

"No you ain't," said the boy sturdily. "I don't want none of your money."

Rather abashed, Harry continued down the street. He tried to present fifty cents to an inebriated man, but a policeman tapped him on the shoulder and told him to move on. He drew up beside a ragged individual and quietly whispered, "Do you wish some money?"

"I'm on," said the tramp, "what's the job?"

"Oh! there's no *job!*" Harry reassured him.

"Tryin' to kid me, hey?" growled the tramp resentfully. "Well, get somebody else." And he slunk off into the crowd.

Next Harry tried to squeeze ten cents into the hand of a passing bellboy, but the youth pulled open his coat and displayed a sign "No Tipping."

With the air of a thief, Harry approached an Italian bootblack, and cautiously deposited ten cents in his hand. At a safe distance he saw the boy wonderingly pocket the dime, and congratulated himself. He had but twenty-four dollars and ninety cents yet to give away! His last success gave him a plan. He stopped at a news-stand where, in full sight of the vender, he dropped a two-dollar bill and sped away in the crowd. After several minutes' hard running he came to a walk amidst the curious glances of the bundle-laden passers-by, and was mentally patting himself on the back when he heard quick breathing behind him, and the very newsie he had just left thrust into his hand the two-dollar bill and was off like a flash.

The perspiration streamed from Harry's forehead and he trudged along despondently. He got rid of twenty-five cents, however, by dropping it into a children's aid slot. He tried to get fifty cents in, but it was a small slot. His first large sum was two dollars to a Salvation Army Santa Claus, and, after this, he kept a sharp lookout for them, but it was past their closing time, and he saw no more of them on his journey.

He was now crossing Union Square, and, after another half hour's patient work, he found himself with only fifteen dollars left to give away. A wet snow was falling which turned to slush as it touched the pavements, and the light dancing pumps he wore were drenched, the water oozing out of his shoe with every step he took. He reached Cooper Square and turned into the Bowery. The number of people on the streets was fast thinning and all around him shops were closing up and their occupants going home. Some boys jeered at him, but, turning up his collar, he plodded on. In his ears rang the saying, mockingly yet kindly, "It is more blessed to give than to receive."

He turned up Third Avenue and counted his remaining money. It amounted to three dollars and seventy cents. Ahead of him he perceived through the thickening snow, two men standing under a lamp post. Here was his chance. He could divide his three dollars and seventy cents between them. He came up to them and tapped one on the shoulder. The man, a thin, ugly looking fellow, turned suspiciously.

"Won't you have some money, you fellow?" he said imperiously, for he was angry at humanity in general and Dorothy in particular. The fellow turned savagely.

"Oh!" he sneered, "you're one of these stiffs tryin' the charity gag, and then gettin' us pulled for beggin'. Come on, Jim, let's show him what we are."

And they showed him. They hit him, they mashed him, they got him down and jumped on him, they broke his hat, they tore his coat. And Harry, gasping, striking, panting, went down in the slush. He thought of the people who had that very night wished him a Merry Christmas. He was certainly having it.

*   *   *   *   *   *   *   *   *   *

Miss Dorothy Harmon closed her book with a snap. It was past eleven and no Harry. What was keeping him? He had probably given up and gone home long ago. With this in mind, she reached up to turn out the light, when suddenly she heard a noise outside as if someone had fallen.

Dorothy rushed to the window and pulled up the blind. There, coming up the steps on his hands and knees was a wretched caricature of a man. He was hatless, coatless, collarless, tieless, and covered with snow. It was Harry. He opened the door and walked into the parlor, leaving a trail of wet snow behind him.

"Well?" he said defiantly.

"Harry," she gasped, "can it be you?"

"Dorothy," he said solemnly, "it is me."

"What—what has happened?"

"Oh, nothing. I've just been giving away that twenty-five dollars." And Harry sat down on the sofa.

"But Harry," she faltered, "your eye is all swollen."

"Oh, my eye? Let me see. Oh, that was on the twenty-second dollar. I had some difficulty with two gentlemen. However, we afterward struck up quite an acquaintance. I had some luck after that. I dropped two dollars in a blind beggar's hat."

"You have been all evening giving away that money?"

"My dear Dorothy, I have decidedly been all evening giving away that money." He rose and brushed a lump of snow from his shoulder. "I really must be going now. I have two—er—friends outside waiting for me." He walked towards the door.

"Two friends?"

"Why—a—they are the two gentlemen I had the difficulty with. They are coming home with me to spend Christmas. They are really nice fellows, though they might seem a trifle rough at first."

Dorothy drew a quick breath. For a minute no one spoke. Then he took her in his arms.

"Dearest," she whispered, "you did this all for me."

A minute later he sprang down the steps, and arm in arm with his friends, walked off in the darkness.

"Good night, Dorothy," he called back, "and a Merry Christmas!"

The Trail of the Duke

It was a hot July night. Inside, through screen, window and door fled the bugs and gathered around the lights like so many humans at a carnival, buzzing, thugging, whirring. From out the night into the houses came the sweltering late summer heat, over-powering and enervating, bursting against the walls and enveloping all mankind like a huge smothering blanket. In the drug stores, the clerks, tired and grumbling handed out ice cream to hundreds of thirsty but misled civilians, while in the corners buzzed the electric fans in a whirring mockery of coolness. In the flats that line upper New York, pianos (sweating ebony perspiration) ground out rag-time tunes of last winter and here and there a wan woman sang the air in a hot soprano. In the tenements, shirt-sleeves gleamed like beacon lights in steady rows along the streets in tiers of from four to eight according to the number of stories of the house. In a word, it was a typical, hot New York summer night.

In his house on upper Fifth Avenue, young Dodson Garland lay on a divan in the billiard room and consumed oceans of mint juleps, as he grumbled at the polo that had kept him in town, the cigarettes, the butler, and occasionally breaking the Second Commandment. The butler ran back and forth with large consignments of juleps and soda and finally, on one of his dramatic entrances, Garland turned towards him and for the first time that evening perceived that the butler was a human being, not a living bottle-tray.

"Hello, Allen," he said, rather surprised that he had made such a discovery. "Are you hot?"

Allen made an expressive gesture with his handkerchief, tried to smile but only succeeded in a feeble, smothery grin.

"Allen," said Garland struck by an inspiration, "what shall I do tonight?" Allen again essayed the grin but, failing once more, sank into a hot, undignified silence.

"Get out of here," exclaimed Garland petulantly, "and bring me another julep and a plate of ice."

"Now," thought the young man, "What shall I do? I can go to the theatre and melt. I can go to a roof-garden and be sung to by a would-be prima donna, or—or go calling." "Go calling," in Garland's vocabulary meant but one thing: to see Mirabel. Mirabel Walmsley was his fiancee since some three months, and was in the city to receive some nobleman or other who was to visit her father. The lucky youth yawned, rolled over, yawned again and rose to a sitting position where he yawned a third time and then got to his feet.

"I'll walk up and see Mirabel. I need a little exercise." And with this final decision he went to his room where he dressed, sweated and dressed, for half an hour. At the end of that time, he emerged from his residence, immaculate, and strolled up Fifth Avenue to Broadway. The city was all outside. As he walked along the white way, he passed groups and groups clad in linen and lingerie, laughing, talking, smoking, smiling, all hot, all uncomfortable.

He reached Mirabel's house and then suddenly stopped on the door step.

"Heavens," he thought, "I forgot all about it. The Duke of Dunsinlane or Artrellane or some lane or other was to arrive today to see Mirabel's papa. Isn't that awful? And I haven't seen Mirabel for three days." He sighed, faltered, and finally walked up the steps and rang the bell. Hardly had he stepped inside the door, when the vision of his dreams came running into the hall in a state of great excitement and perturbation.

"Oh, Doddy!" she burst out, "I'm in an awful situation. "The Duke went out of the house an hour ago. None of the maids saw him go. He just wandered out. You must find him. He's probably lost—lost and nobody knows him." Mirabel wrung her hands in entrancing despair. "Oh, I shall die if he's lost—and it so hot. He'll have a sunstroke surely or a—moonstroke. Go and find him. We've telephoned the police, but it won't do any good. Hurry up! Do! oh, Doddy, I'm so nervous."

"Doddy" put his hands in his pockets, sighed, put his hat on his head and sighed again. Then he turned towards the door. Mirabel, her face anxious, followed him.

"Bring him right up here if you find him. Oh Doddy you're a life-saver. The life-saver sighed again and walked quickly through the portal. On the door-step he paused.

"Well, of all outrageous things! To hunt for a French Duke in New York. This is outrageous. Where shall I go? What will I do. He paused at the door-step and then, following the crowd, strode toward Broadway. "Now let me see. I must have a plan of action. I can't go up and ask everybody I meet if he's the Duke of ———, well of, well—I can't remember his name. I don't know what he looks like. He probably can't talk English. Oh, curses on the nobility."

He strode aimlessly, hot and muddled. He wished he had asked Mirabel the Duke's name and personal appearance, but it was now too late. He would not convict himself of such a blunder. Reaching Broadway he suddenly bethought himself of a plan of action.

"I'll try the restaurants." He started down towards Sherry's and had gone but half a block when he had an inspiration. The Duke's picture was in some evening paper, and his name, too.

He bought a paper and sought for the picture with no result. He tried again and again. On his seventh paper he found it: "The Duke of Matterlane Visits American Millionaire."

The Duke, a man with side whiskers and eye-glasses stared menacingly at him from the paper. Garland heaved a sigh of relief, took a long look at the likeness and stuck the paper into his pocket.

"Now to business," he muttered, wiping his drenched brow, "Duke or die."

Five minutes later he entered Sherry's, where he sat down and ordered ginger ale. There was the usual summer night crowd, listless, flushed, and sunburned. There was the usual champagne and ice that seemed hotter than the room; but there was no Duke. He sighed, rose, and visited Delmonico's, Martin's, at each place consuming a glass of ginger ale.

"I'll have to cut out the drinking," he thought, "or I'll be inebriated by the time I find his royal nuisance."

On his weary trail, he visited more restaurants and more hotels, ever searching; sometimes thinking he saw an oasis and finding. it only a mirage. He had consumed so much ginger ale that he felt a swaying sea-sickness as he walked; yet he plodded on, hotter and hotter, uncomfortable, and, as Alice in Wonderland would have said, uncomfortabler. His mind was grimly and tenaciously set on the Duke's face. As he walked along, from hotel to cafe, from cafe to restaurant, the Duke's whiskers remained glued firmly to the insides of his brains. It was half past eight by the City Hall clock when he started on his quest. It was now quarter past ten, hotter, sultrier and stuffier than ever. He had visited every important place of refreshment. He tried the drug stores. He went to four theatres and had the Duke paged, at a large bribe. His money was getting low, his spirits were lower still; but his temperature soared majestically and triumphantly aloft.

Finally, passing through an alley which had been recommended to him as a short cut, he saw before him a man lighting a cigarette. By the flickering match he noticed the whiskers. He stopped dead in his tracks, afraid that it might not be the Duke. The man lit another cigarette. Sure enough, the sideburns, eyeglasses and the whole face proved the question without a doubt.

Garland walked towards the man. The man looked back at him and started to walk in the opposite direction. Garland started to run; the man looked over his shoulder and started to run also. Garland slowed down. The man slowed down. They emerged upon Broadway in the same relative position and the man started north. Forty feet behind, in stolid determination, walked Garland without his hat. He had left it in the alley.

For eight blocks they continued, the man behind being the pacemaker. Then the Duke spoke quietly to a policeman and when Garland, lost in an obsession of pursuit, was grabbed by the arm by a blue-coated Gorgas, he saw ahead of him the Duke start to run. In a frenzy he struck at the policeman and stunned him. He ran on and in three blocks he had made up what he had lost. For five more blocks the Duke continued, glancing now and then over his shoulder. On the sixth block he stopped. Garland approached him with steady step. He of the side whiskers was standing under a lamp post. Garland came up and put his hand on his shoulder.

"Your Grace."

"What's dat?" said the Duke, with an unmistakable east-side accent. Garland was staggered.

"I'll grace you," continued the side burns aggressively. "I saw you was a swell and I'd a dropped you bad only I'm just out of jail myself. Now listen here. I'll give you two seconds to get scarce. Go on, beat it."

Garland beat it. Crestfallen and broken-hearted he walked away and set off for Mirabel's. He would at least make a decent ending to a miserable quest. A half an hour later he rang the bell, his clothes hanging on him like a wet bathing suit.

Mirabel came to the door cool and fascinating.

"Oh Doddy," she exclaimed. "Thank you so much. Dukey," and she held up a small white poodle which she had in her arms, "came back ten minutes after you left. He had just followed the mail man."

Garland sat down on the step.

"But the Duke of Matterlane?"

"Oh," said Mirabel, "he comes tomorrow. You must come right over and meet him."

"Im afraid I can't," said Garland, rising feebly, "previous engagement." He paused, smiled faintly and set off across the sultry moon-lit pavement.

Pain and the Scientist

Walter Hamilton Bartney moved to Middleton because it was quiet and offered him an opportunity of studying law, which he should have done long ago. He chose a quiet house rather out in the suburbs of the village, for as he reasoned to himself, "Middleton is a suburb and remarkably quiet at that. Therefore a suburb of a suburb must be the very depth of solitude, and that is what I want." So Bartney chose a small house in the suburbs and settled down. There was a vacant lot on his left, and on his right Skiggs, the famous Christian Scientist. It is because of Skiggs that this story was written.

Bartney, like the very agreeable young man he was, decided that it would be only neighborly to pay Skiggs a visit, not that he was very much interested in the personality of Mr. Skiggs, but because he had never seen a real Christian Scientist and he felt that his life would be empty without the sight of one.

However, he chose a most unlucky time for his visit. It was one night, dark as pitch that, feeling restless, he set off as the clock struck ten to investigate and become acquainted. He strode out of his lot and along the path that went by name of a road, feeling his way between bushes and rocks and keeping his eye on the solitary light that burned in Mr. Skiggs' house.

"It would be blamed unlucky for me if he should take a notion to turn out that light," he muttered through his clenched teeth. "I'd be lost. I'd just have to sit down and wait until morning."

He approached the house, felt around cautiously, and, reaching for what he thought was a step, uttered an exclamation of pain, for a large stone had rolled down over his leg and pinned him to the earth. He grunted, swore, and tried to move the rock, but he was held powerless by the huge stone, and his efforts were unavailing.

"Hello!" he shouted. "Mr. Skiggs!"

There was no answer.

"Help, in there," he cried again, "Help!"

A light was lit upstairs and a head, topped with a conical shaped night-cap, poked itself out of the window like an animated jack-in-the-box.

"Who's there?" said the night-cap in a high-pitched querulous voice. "Who's there? Speak, or I fire."

"Don't fire! It's me—Bartney, your neighbor. I've had an accident, a nasty ankle wrench, and there's a stone on top of me."

"Bartney?" queried the night cap, nodding pensively. "Who's Bartney?"

Bartney swore inwardly.

"I'm your neighbor. I live next door. This stone is very heavy. If you would come down here—"

"How do I know you're Bartney, whoever he is?" demanded the night cap. "How do I know you won't get me out there and blackjack me?"

"For heaven's sake," cried Bartney, "look and see. Turn a searchlight on me, and see if I'm not pinned down."

"I have no searchlight," came the voice from above.

"Then you'll have to take a chance. I can't stay here all night."

"Then go away. I am not stopping you," said the night cap with a decisive squeak in his voice.

"Mr. Skiggs," said Bartney in desperation, "I am in mortal agony and—"

"You are not in mortal agony," announced Mr. Skiggs.

"What? Do you still think I'm trying to entice you out here to murder you?"

"I repeat, you are not in mortal agony. I am convinced now that you really think you are hurt, but I assure you, you are not."

"He's crazy," thought Bartney.

"I shall endeavor to prove to you that you are not, thus causing you more relief than I would if I lifted the stone. I am very moderate. I will treat you now at the rate of three dollars an hour."

"An hour?" shouted Bartney fiercely. "You come down here and roll this stone off me, or I'll skin you alive!"

"Even against your will," went on Mr. Skiggs. "I feel called upon to treat you, for it is a duty to everyone to help the injured, or rather those who fancy themselves injured. Now, clear your mind of all sensation, and we will begin the treatment."

"Come down here, you mean, low-browed fanatic!" yelled Bartney, forgetting his pain in a paroxysm of rage. "Come down here, and I'll drive every bit of Christian Science out of your head."

"To begin with," began the shrill falsetto from the window, "there is no pain—absolutely none. Do you begin to have an inkling of that?"

"No," shouted Bartney. "You, you—" his voice was lost in a gurgle of impotent rage.

"Now, all is mind. Mind is everything. Matter is nothing—absolutely nothing. You are well. You fancy you are hurt, but you are not."

"You lie," shrieked Bartney.

Unheeding, Mr. Skiggs went on.

"Thus, if there is no pain, it can not act on your mind. A sensation is not physical. If you had no brain, there would be no pain, for what you call pain acts on the brain. You see?"

"Oh-h," cried Bartney, "if you saw what a bottomless well of punishment you were digging for yourself, you'd cut out that monkey business."

"Therefore, as so-called pain is a mental sensation, your ankle doesn't hurt you. Your brain may imagine it does, but all sensation goes to the brain. You are very foolish when you complain of hurt—"

Bartney's patience wore out. He drew in his breath, and let out a yell that echoed and re-echoed through the night air. He

repeated it again and again, and at length he heard the sound
of footsteps coming up the road.

"Hello!" came a voice.

Bartney breathed a prayer of thanksgiving.

"Come here! I've had an accident," he called, and a minute
later the night watchman's brawny arms had rolled the stone off
him, and he staggered to his feet.

"Good night," called the Christian Scientist sweetly. "I hope
I have made some impression on you."

"You certainly have," called back Bartney as he limped off, his
hand on the watchman's shoulder, "one I won't forget."

Two days later, as Bartney sat with his foot on a pillow he
pulled an unfamiliar envelope out of his mail and opened it. It
read:

WILLIAM BARTNEY.

To HEPEZIA SKIGGS, DR.

Treatment by Christian Science—$3.00. Payment by check
or money order.

*   *   *   *   *   *   *   *   *   *

The weeks wore on. Bartney was up and around. Out in his
yard he started a flower garden and became a floral enthusiast.
Every day he planted, and the next day he would weed what
he had planted. But it gave him something to do, for law was
tiresome at times.

One bright summer's day, he left his house and strolled towards
the garden, where the day before he had planted in despair some
"store bought" pansies. He perceived to his surprise a long, thin,
slippery-looking figure bending over, picking his new acquisitions.
With quiet tread he approached, and, as the invader turned
around, he said severely:

"What are you doing, sir?"

"I was plucking-er-a few posies—"

The long, thin, slippery looking figure got no further. Though
the face had been strange to Bartney, the voice, a thin, querelous

falsetto, was one he would never forget. He advanced slowly, eyeing the owner of that voice, as the wolf eyes his prey.

"Well, Mr. Skiggs, how is it I find you on my property?"

Mr. Skiggs appeared unaccountably shy and looked the other way.

"I repeat," said Bartney, "that I find you here on my property —and in my power."

"Yes, sir," said Mr. Skiggs, squirming in alarm.

Bartney grabbed him by the collar, and shook him as a terrier does a rat.

"You conceited imp of Christian Science! You miserable hypocrite! What?" he demanded fiercely, as Skiggs emitted a cry of protest. "You yell. How dare you? Don't you know there is no such thing as pain? Come on, now, give me some of that Christian Science. Say 'mind is everything. Say it!'"

'Mr. Skiggs, in the midst of his jerky course, said quaveringly, "Mind is everyth-thing."

"Pain is nothing," urged his tormenter grimly.

"P-Pain is nothing," repeated Mr. Skiggs feelingly.

The shaking continued.

"Remember, Skiggs, this is all for the good of the cause. I hope you're taking it to heart. Remember, such is life, therefore life is such. Do you see?"

He left off shaking, and proceeded to entice Skiggs around by a grip on his collar, the scientist meanwhile kicking and struggling violently.

"Now," said Bartney, "I want you to assure me that you feel no pain. Go on, do it!"

"I f-feel—ouch," he exclaimed as he passed over a large stone is his course, "n-no pain."

"Now," said Bartney, "I want two dollars for the hours' Christian Science treatment I have given you. Out with it."

Skiggs hesitated, but the look of Bartney's eyes and a tightening of Bartney's grip convinced him, and he unwillingly tendered a bill. Bartney tore it to pieces and distributed the fragments to the wind.

"Now, you may go."

Skiggs, when his collar was released, took to his heels, and his flying footsteps crossed the boundary line in less time than you would imagine.

"Good-bye, Mr. Skiggs," called Bartney pleasantly. "Any other time you want a treatment come over. The price is always the same. I see you know one thing I didn't have to teach you. There's no such thing as pain, when somebody else is the goat."

Shadow Laurels

Fitzgerald's literary career at Princeton, where, besides fiction, he wrote fifty-five musical comedy lyrics, several poems, parodies, and book reviews, and where he became secretary of the Triangle Club and an editor of the *Tiger* and *The Nassau Literary Magazine*, may be divided into two phases, the first extending from matriculation (September, 1913) to initial departure (December, 1915) and the second from readmittance (September, 1916) to final departure (November, 1917). During the earlier of these, he contributed the plot and lyrics to one Triangle Club show, lyrics to another, and composed "Shadow Laurels" (printed April, 1915), while publishing but a single story, "The Ordeal" (June, 1915). During the later phase, however, he published five stories in *The Nassau Literary Magazine*—"The Spire and the Gargoyle" (February, 1917), "Tarquin of Cheepside" (April, 1917), "Babes in the Woods" (May, 1917), "Sentiment—and the Use of Rouge" (June, 1917), "The Pierian Springs and the Last Straw" (October, 1917)—while contributing lyrics to only one Triangle Club show and composing "The Debutante" (printed January, 1917).

Henry Dan Piper has summarized the immediate critical reception of the author's college fiction:

It was a chastened Fitzgerald who returned to Princeton in September, 1916, to begin junior year all over again. Instead of writing for Triangle and the *Tiger*, he now turned to the more serious pages of the *Nassau Literary Magazine*. There was at least a story, and a poem or a book review, in every issue. It was the stories, especially, which announced the emergence of a new and

impressive talent. Prominent critics like Katharine Fullerton
Gerould and William Rose Benét, for instance, singled out
Fitzgerald's fiction for special praise in the reviews of *Lit* issues they
wrote for *The Daily Princetonian*. Moreover, when Fitzgerald sent
one of his stories to H. L. Mencken, editor of *The Smart Set*
magazine, Mencken wrote back enthusiastically asking to see more
of his works. . . .

Most significant of all this acclaim, however, was the response
his *Nassau Lit* stories elicited from his own contemporaries. Edi-
tors of literary magazines on other Eastern college campuses discovered his stories with the shock of recognition and praised them
vigorously in their editorial columns. Here as early as 1917 is evidence already of Fitzgerald's special gift for voicing the feelings
and attitudes of his own generation then just coming of age—a
gift which by 1920 would be nationally famous. ("Scott Fitzgerald's Prep-School Writings," *The Princeton University Library
Chronicle*, Autumn, 1955)

"Shadow Laurels" dramatizes the author's ambivalent attitude
toward his father. The wealthy Jacques Chandelle, who embodies
the would-be Scott Fitzgerald, describes Jean Chandelle, who resembles the actual Edward Fitzgerald, thus: "a little man with a
black beard, terribly lazy—the only good I ever remember his
doing was to teach me to read and write." Years later the real
son would remember a great deal more that had been good, as
the handwritten document "The Death of My Father" * proves:

Convention would make me preface this with an apology for
the lack of taste of discussing an emotion so close to me. But all
my criterions of taste dissapeared when on the advice of a fairy
I read Mrs Emily Price Posts' Book of Etiquette some months
ago. Up to that time I had always thought of myself as an American gentleman, somewhat crazy and often desperate and bad but

* Material in brackets was crossed out by Fitzgerald. See Appendix
for facsimile of this document, which gives some indication of the
alterations and insertions made by Fitzgerald.

partaking of the sensativity of my race and class and and with
out much a record of many times having injured the strong but
never the weak. But now I don't know—the mixture of the obvious and the snobbish in that book—and its an honest book, a
frank piece of worldly wisdom written for the new women of the
bull market—has sent me back again to all the things I felt at
twenty. I kept wondering all through it how Mrs Post would have
thought of my my father.

I loved my father—always deep in my subconscious I have referred judgements back to him, what he would have thought, or
done. He loved me—and felt a deep responsibility for me—I was
born several months after the sudden death of my two elder sisters
& he felt what the effect this would be on my mother, that he
would be my only moral guide. He became that to the best of
his ability. He came from tired old stock with very little left of
vitality and mental energy but he managed to raise a little for
me. [We walked down town in the Summer to have our shoes
shined me in my sailor suit and father in his always beautifully
cut clothes and he told me the few things I ever learned about
life until a few years later from] a catholic priest, Monsignor
Fay. What he knew he had learned from his mother & grandmother, the latter a bore to me—"If your grandmother Scott heard
that she would turn over in her grave." What he told me were
simple things, [like
"Once when I went in a room as a young man. I was confused
so I went up to the oldest woman there and introduced myself
and afterwards the people of that town always thought I had good
manners" He did that from a good heart that came from another America—he was much too sure of what he was, much too
sure of the deep pride of the two proud women who brought
him up to doubt for a moment that his own instincts were
good]— It was a horror to find the natural gesture expressed with
cynical distortion in Mrs Price Posts book.

We walked down town in Buffalo on Sunday mornings &
my white ducks were stiff with starch & he was very proud walking with his handsome little boy. We had our shoes shined and

he lit his cigar and we bought the Sunday papers. When I was a little older I did not understand at all why men that I knew were vulgar and not gentlemen made him stand up or give the better chair on our verandah. But I know now. There was new young peasant stock coming up every ten years & he was of the generation of the colonies and the revolution.

Once he hit me. I called him a liar—I was about thirteen I think & I said if he called me a liar he was a liar. He hit me—he had spanked me before & always with good reason—but this time there was ill feeling & we were both sorry for years. I think though we didn't say anything to each other. Later we used to have awful rows on political subjects on which we violently agreed but we never came to the point of personal animosity about them but if things came to fever heat the one most affected quitted the arena, left the room.

[I don't see how all this could possibly interest anyone but me]

I ran away when I was seven on the fourth of July—I spent the day with a friend in a pear orchard & the police were informed that I was missing and on my return my father thrashed me according to the custom of the nineties—on the bottom and then, let me come out and watch the night fireworks from the balcony with my pants still down & my behind smarting & knowing in my heart that he was absolutely right. Afterwards, seeing in his face his regret that it had to happen I asked him to tell me a story. I knew what it would be—he had only a few, the Story of the Spy, the one about the Man Hung by his Thumbs, the one about Earlys March.

Do you want to hear them. I'm so tired of them all that I can't make them interesting. But maybe they are because I used to ask father to repeat & repeat & repeat. (The F. Scott Fitzgerald Papers)

Shadow Laurels

(*The scene is the interior of a wine shop in Paris. The walls are lined on all sides by kegs, piled like logs. The ceiling is low and covered with cobwebs. The midafternoon sun filters dejectedly through the one-barred window at the back. Doors are on both sides; one, heavy and powerful, opens outside; the other, on the left, leads to some inner chamber. A large table stands in the middle of the room backed by smaller ones set around the walls. A ship's lamp hangs above the main table.*

As the curtain rises there is knocking at the outside door—rather impatient knocking—and almost immediately Pitou, the wine dealer, enters from the other room and shuffles toward the door. He is an old man with unkempt beard and dirty corduroys.)

Pitou—Coming, coming—Hold tight! (*The knocking stops. Pitou unlatches the door and it swings open. A man in a top hat and opera cloak enters. Jaques Chandelle is perhaps thirty-seven, tall and well groomed. His eyes are clear and penetrating, his chin, clean shaven, is sharp and decisive. His manner is that of a man accustomed only to success but ready and willing to work hard in any emergency. He speaks French with an odd accent as of one who knew the language well in early years but whose accent had grown toneless through long years away from France.*)

Pitou—Good afternoon, Monsieur.

Chandelle—(*looking about him curiously*) Are you perhaps Monsieur Pitou?

Pitou—Yes, Monsieur.

Chandelle—Ah! I was told that one would always find you in at this hour. (*He takes off his overcoat and lays it carefully on a chair*) I was told also that you could help me.

69

Pitou—(*puzzled*) I could help you?

Chandelle—(*Sitting down wearily on a wooden chair near the table*) Yes, I'm a—a stranger in the city—now. I'm trying to trace someone—someone who has been dead many years. I've been informed that you're the oldest inhabitant (*he smiles faintly.*)

Pitou—(*rather pleased*) Perhaps—and yet there are older than I, ah yes, older than I. (*He sits down across the table from Chandelle.*)

Chandelle—And so I came for you. (*He bends earnestly over the table toward Pitou.*) Monsieur Pitou, I am trying to trace my father.

Pitou—Yes.

Chandelle—He died in this district about twenty years ago.

Pitou—Monsieur's father was murdered?

Chandelle—Good God, no! What makes you think that?

Pitou—I thought perhaps in this district twenty years ago, an aristocrat—

Chandelle—My father was no aristocrat. As I remember, his last position was that of waiter in some forgotten café. (*Pitou glances at Chandelle's clothes and looks mystified.*) Here I'll explain. I left France twenty-eight years ago to go to the states with my uncle. We went over in an immigrant ship, if you know what that is.

Pitou—Yes: I know.

Chandelle—My parents remained in France. The last I remember of my father was that he was a little man with a black beard, terribly lazy—the only good I ever remember his doing was to teach me to read and write. Where he picked up that accomplishment I don't know. Five years after we reached America we ran across some newly landed French from this part of the city, who said that both my parents were dead. Soon after that my uncle died and I was far too busy to worry over parents whom I had half forgotten anyway. (*He pauses.*) Well to cut it short I prospered and—

Pitou—(*deferentially*) Monsieur is rich—'tis strange—'tis very strange.

Chandelle—Pitou, it probably appears strange to you that I should burst in on you now at this time of life, looking for traces of a father who went completely out of my life over twenty years ago.

Pitou—Oh—I understood you to say he was dead.

Chandelle—Yes he's dead, but (*hesitates*) Pitou, I wonder if you can understand if I tell you why I am here.

Pitou—Yes, perhaps.

Chandelle—(*very earnestly*) Monsieur Pitou, in America the men I see now, the women I know all had fathers, fathers to be ashamed of, fathers to be proud of, fathers in gilt frames, and fathers in the family closet, Civil War fathers, and Ellis Island fathers. Some even had grandfathers.

Pitou—I had a grandfather. I remember.

Chandelle—(*interrupting*) I want to see people who knew him, who had talked with him. I want to find out his intelligence, his life, his record. (*Impetuously*) I want to sense him—I want to know him—

Pitou—(interrupting) What was his name?

Chandelle—Chandelle, Jean Chandelle.

Pitou—(*quietly*) I knew him.

Chandelle—You knew him?

Pitou—He came here often to drink—that was long ago when this place was the rendezvous of half the district.

Chandelle—(*excitedly*) Here? He used to come here? To this room? Good Lord, the very house he lived in was torn down ten years ago. In two days' search you are the first soul I've found who knew him. Tell me of him—everything—be frank.

Pitou—Many come and go in forty years (*shakes his head.*) There are many names and many faces—Jean Chandelle—ah, of course, Jean Chandelle. Yes, yes; the chief fact I can remember about your father was that he was a—a—

Chandelle—Yes.

Pitou—A terrible drunkard.

Chandelle—A drunkard—I expected as much. (*He looks a trifle downcast, but makes a half-hearted attempt not to show it.*)

Pitou—(*Rambling on through a sea of reminiscence*) I remember one Sunday night in July—hot night—baking—your father—let's see—your father tried to knife Pierre Courru for drinking his mug of sherry.

Chandelle—Ah!

Pitou—And then—ah, yes, (*excitedly standing up*) I see it again. Your father is playing *vingt-et-un* and they say he is cheating so he breaks Clavine's shin with a chair and throws a bottle at someone and Lafouquet sticks a knife into his lung. He never got over that. That was—was two years before he died.

Chandelle—So he cheated and was murdered. My God, I've crossed the ocean to discover that.

Pitou—No—no—I never believed he cheated. They were laying for him—

Chandelle—(*burying his face in his hands*) Is that all (*he shrugs his shoulders; his voice is a trifle broken*) I scarcely expected a—saint but—well: so he was a rotler.

Pitou—(*Laying his hand on Chandelle's shoulder*) There Monsieur, I have talked too much. Those were rough days. Knives were drawn at anything. Your father—but hold—do you want to meet three friends of his, his best friends. They can tell you much more than I.

Chandelle—(*gloomily*) His friends?

Pitou—(*reminiscent again*) There were four of them. Three come here yet—will be here this afternoon—your father was the fourth and they would sit at this table and talk and drink. They talked nonsense—everyone said; the wine room poked fun at them —called them "les Académiciens Ridicules." Night after night would they sit there. They would slouch in at eight and stagger out at twelve—

(*The door swings open and three men enter. The first, Lamarque, is a tall man, lean and with a thin straggly beard. The second, Destage, is short and fat, white bearded and bald. The third, Francois Meridien is slender, with black hair streaked with grey and a small moustache. His face is pitifully weak, his eyes small, his chin sloping. He is very nervous. They all glance with dumb curiosity at Chandelle.*)

Pitou—(*including all three with a sweep of his arm*) Here they are, Monsieur, they can tell you more than I. (*Turning to the others*) Messieurs, this gentleman desires to know about—

Chandelle—(*rising hastily and interrupting Pitou*) About a friend of my father's. Pitou tells me you knew him. I believe his name was—Chandelle.

(*The three men start and Francois begins to laugh nervously.*)

Lamarque—(*after a pause*) Chandelle?

Francois—Jean Chandelle? So he had another friend besides us?

Destage—You will pardon me, Monsieur: that name—no one but us had mentioned it for twenty-two years.

Lamarque—(*trying to be dignified, but looking a trifle ridiculous*) And with us it is mentioned with reverence and awe.

Destage—Lamarque exaggerates a little perhaps. (*Very seriously*) He was very dear to us. (*Again Francois laughs nervously.*)

Lamarque—But what is it that Monsieur wishes to know? (*Chandelle motions them to sit down. They take places at the big table and Destage produces a pipe and begins to fill it.*)

Francois—Why, we're four again!

Lamarque—Idiot!

Chandelle—Here, Pitou! Wine for everyone. (*Pitou nods and shuffles out*) Now, Messieurs, tell me of Chandelle. Tell me of his personality.

(*Lamarque looks blankly at Destage.*)

Destage—Well, he was—was attractive—

Lamarque—Not to everyone.

Destage—But to us. Some thought him a sneak. (*Chandelle winces*) He was a wonderful talker—when he wished, he could amuse the whole wine room. But he preferred to talk to us. (*Pitou enters with a bottle and glasses. He pours and leaves the bottle on the table. Then he goes out.*)

Lamarque—He was educated. God knows how.

Francois—(*draining his glass and pouring out more.*) He knew everything, he could tell anything—he used to tell me poetry. Oh, what poetry! And I would listen and dream—

Destage—And he could make verses and sing them with his guitar.

Lamarque—And he would tell us about men and women of history—about Charlotte Corday and Fouquet and Moliére and St. Louis and Mamine, the strangler, and Charlemagne and Mme. Dubarry and Machiavelli and John Law and Francois Villon—

Destage—Villon! (*enthusiastically*) He loved Villon. He would talk for hours of him.

Francois—(*Pouring more wine*) And then he would get very drunk and say "Let us fight" and he would stand on the table and say that everyone in the wine shop was a pig and a son of pigs. La! He would grab a chair or a table and Sacré Vie Dieu! but those were hard nights for us.

Lamarque—Then he would take his hat and guitar and go into the streets to sing. He would sing about the moon.

Francois—And the roses and the ivory towers of Babylon and about the ancient ladies of the court and about "the silent chords that flow from the ocean to the moon."

Destage—That's why he made no money. He was bright and clever—when we worked, he worked feverishly hard, but he was always drunk, night and day.

Lamarque—Often he lived on liquor alone for weeks at a time.

Destage—He was much in jail toward the end.

Chandelle—(*calling*) Pitou! More wine!

Francois—(*excitedly*) And me! He used to like me best. He used to say that I was a child and he would train me. He died before he began. (*Pitou enters with another bottle of wine; Francois siezes it eagerly and pours himself a glass.*)

Destage—And then that cursed Lafouquet—stuck him with a knife.

Francois—But I fixed Lafouquet. He stood on the Seine bridge drunk and—

Lamarque—Shut up, you fool you—

Francois—I pushed him and he sank—down—down—and that night Chandelle came in a dream and thanked me.

Chandelle—(*shuddering*) How long—for how many years did you come here.

Destage—Six or seven. (*Gloomily*) Had to end—had to end.

Chandelle—And he's forgotten. He left nothing. He'll never be thought of again.

Destage—Remembered! Bah! Posterity is as much a charlatan as the most prejudiced tragic critic that ever boot-licked an actor. (*He turns his glass nervously round and round*) You don't realize—I'm afraid—how we feel about Jean Chandelle, Francois and Lamarque and I—he was more than a genius to be admired—

Francois—(*hoarsely*) Don't you see, he stood for us as well as for himself.

Lamarque—(*rising excitedly and walking up and down.*) There we were—four men—three of us poor dreamers—artistically educated, practically illiterate (*he turns savagely to Chandelle and speaks almost menacingly*) Do you realize that I can neither read nor write. Do you realize that back of Francois there, despite his fine phrases, there is a character weak as water, a mind as shallow as—

(*Francois starts up angrily.*)

Lemarque—Sit down (*Francois sits down muttering.*)

Francois—(*after a pause*) But, Monsieur, you must know—I leave the gift of—of—(*helplessly*) I can't name it—appreciation, artistic, aesthetic sense—call it what you will. Weak—yes, why not? Here I am, with no chance, the world against me. I lie—I steal perhaps—I am drunk—I—

(*Destage fills up Francois glass with wine.*)

Destage—Here! Drink that and shut up! You are boring the gentleman. There is his weak side—poor infant.

(*Chandelle who has listened to the last, keenly turns his chair toward Destage.*)

Chandelle—But you say my father was more to you than a personal friend; in what way?

Lamarque—Can't you see?

Francois—I—I—he helped—(*Destage pours out more wine and gives it to him.*)

Destage—You see he—how shall I say it?—he expressed us. If you can imagine a mind like mine, potently lyrical, sensitive without being cultivated. If you can imagine what a balm, what a medicine, what an all in all was summed up for me in my conversations with him. It was everything to me. I would struggle pathetically for a phrase to express a million yearnings and he would say it in a word.

Lamarque—Monsieur is bored? (*Chandelle shakes his head and opening his case selects a cigarette and lights it.*)

Lamarque—Here, sir, are three rats, the product of a sewer—destined by nature to live and die in the filthy ruts where they were born. But these three rats in one thing are not of the sewer—they have eyes. Nothing to keep them from remaining in the sewer but their eyes, nothing to help them if they go out but their eyes—and now here comes the light. And it came and passed and left us rats again—vile rats—and one, when he lost the light, went blind.

Francois—(*muttering to himself*)—

Blind! Blind! Blind!
Then he ran alone, when the light had passed;
The sun had set and the night fell fast;
The rat lay down in the sewer at last,
Blind!

(*A beam of the sunset has come to rest on the glass of wine that Francois holds in his hand. The wine glitters and sparkles. Francois looks at it, starts, and drops the glass. The wine runs over the table.*)

Destage—(*animatedly*) Fifteen—twenty years ago he sat where you sat, small, heavy-bearded, black eyed—always sleepy looking.

Francois—(*his eyes closed—his voice trailing off*) Always sleepy, sleepy, slee—

Chandelle—(*dreamily*) He was a poet unsinging, crowned with wreaths of ashes. (*His voice rings with just a shade of triumph.*)

Francois—(*talking in his sleep*) Ah, well Chandelle, are you witty to-night, or melancholy or stupid or drunk.

Chandelle—Messieurs—it grows late. I must be off. Drink, all of you (*enthusiastically*) Drink until you cannot talk or walk or see. (*He throws a bill on the table.*)

Destage—Young Monsieur?

(*Chandelle dons his coat and hat. Pitou enters with more wine. He fills the glasses.*)

Lamarque—Drink with us, Monsieur.

Francois—(*asleep*) Toast, Chandelle, toast.

Chandelle—(*taking a glass and raising it aloft*). Toast (*His face is a little red and his hand unsteady. He appears infinitely more gallic than when he entered the wine shop.*)

Chandelle—I drink to one who might have been all, who was nothing—who might have sung; who only listened—who might have seen the sun; who but watched a dying ember—who drank of gall and wore a wreath of shadow laurels—

(*The others have risen, even Francois who totters wildly forward.*)

Francois—Jean, Jean, don't go—don't—till I, Francois—you can't leave me—I'll be all alone—alone—alone (*his voice rises higher and higher*) My God, man, can't you see, you have no right to die—You are my soul. (*He stands for a moment, then sprawls across the table. Far away in the twilight a violin sighs plaintively. The last beam of the sun rests on Francois' head. Chandelle opens the door and goes out.*)

Destage—The old days go by, and the old loves and the old spirit. "Ou sont les neiges d'antan?" I guess. (*Pauses unsteadily and then continues.*) I've gone far enough without him.

Lamarque—(*dreamily*) Far enough.

Destage—Your hand Jaques! (*They clasp hands*).

Francois—(*wildly*) Here—I, too—you won't leave me (*feebly*) I want—just one more glass—one more—

(*The light fades and disappears.*)

(CURTAIN.)

The Ordeal

Scott Fitzgerald was brought up a Roman Catholic in a family Archbishop Dowling of St. Paul once described as "staunch, devout, generous." (The F. Scott Fitzgerald Papers) We know that, besides his father, Monsignor Sigourney Webster Fay, who became headmaster at the Newman School and Monsignor Darcy of *This Side of Paradise*, exerted some influence on him. Arthur Mizener has said Fay appealed to Fitzgerald because he was "a man of taste and cultivation . . . an eighteen-nineties aesthete, a dandy" and financially well-to-do. (*The Far Side of Paradise*, p. 42) The appeal seems to have been reciprocal, for Fay's letters of 1918, which discuss intellectual and literary matters knowingly and which were incorporated in the novel almost verbatim, express interest and sympathy. He signed himself, "Your affectionate but somewhat irate Father" and referred to his "paternal arms." He claimed that both of them feared Satan, that neither would rid himself of the fear of God; yet he also observed that the "mystical element" in both explained "the secret of our success." (The F. Scott Fitzgerald Papers) Only one thing did Fitzgerald ever attribute directly to Fay, however: he "made of that church a dazzling, golden thing, dispelling its oppressive mugginess and giving the succession of days upon gray days, passing under its plaintive ritual, the romantic glamour of an adolescent dream." (Review of *The Oppidian*, by Shane Leslie, *New York Tribune*, May 14, 1922)

Whatever Monsignor Fay's influence was, it was not sufficient to prevent his protégé from deserting Roman Catholicism. In *This Side of Paradise*, the hero admits that despite the fact that the mob

78

needs someone crying, "Thou shalt not!" and that the Church represents "the only assimilative, traditionary bulwark against the decay of morals," he cannot accept it. (p. 303) The war rather than making him religious has made him "a passionate agnostic." Neither Roman Catholicism nor the other religions were equipped to meet the exigencies of the time, according to Scott Fitzgerald. A generation had "grown up to find all Gods dead, all wars fought, all faiths in man shaken." (*Ibid.*) He wrote to Edmund Wilson in 1920: "I am ashamed to say that my Catholicism is scarcely more than a memory—no that's wrong. it's more than that; at any rate I go not to the church nor mumble stray nothings over chrystaline beads." (*The Crack-Up*, New York, 1956, p. 254) By 1940 he felt Communism and Catholicism to be equally fanatical and equally obdurate. The Roman Catholic Church exhibited strong feelings toward him too, for he was refused burial in consecrated ground.

"The Ordeal," which is the single work of fiction composed between "The Trail of the Duke" (1913) and "The Spire and the Gargoyle" (1917), provided the basis for another story, "Benediction," which appeared during 1920 in both *The Smart Set* and *Flappers and Philosophers* (New York, pp. 194-218). While "Benediction" retained the settings of "The Ordeal," and, like the earlier piece, grew out of a visit Fitzgerald made to a novice at the Jesuit Seminary in Woodstock, Maryland, it actually borrowed very little. The protagonist, a nineteen-year-old blonde pays a visit to her thirty-six-year-old brother, whom she has not seen in fourteen years. Although a persuasive Jesuit, he fails to draw her away from a pending love affair. The following passage should indicate where the doubts voiced in "The Ordeal" would soon lead Fitzgerald:

> "I don't want to shock you, Kieth, but I can't tell you how—how inconvenient being a Catholic is. It really doesn't seem to apply any more. As far as morals go, some of the wildest boys I know are Catholics. And the brightest boys—I mean the ones

who think and read a lot, don't seem to believe in much of anything any more." . . .

"You can't shock a monk. He's a professional shock-absorber."

"Well," she continued, "that's about all. It seems so—so *narrow*. Church schools, for instance. There's more freedom about things that Catholic people can't see—like birth control."

On November 16, 1920, Fitzgerald complained to Shane Leslie, a young Irish author: "Do you know that the story 'Benediction' that I sent you and that also received the imprimatur of the most intelligent priest I know has come in for the most terrible lashing from the American Catholic intelligentsia? It's too much for me. It seems that an Englishman like Benson can write anything but an American had better have his works either pious tracts for nuns or else disassociate them from the church as a living issue." (*The Letters of F. Scott Fitzgerald*, p. 378)

The Ordeal

The hot four o'clock sun beat down familiarly upon the wide stretch of Maryland country, burning up the long valleys, powdering the winding road into fine dust and glaring on the ugly slated roof of the monastery. Into the gardens it poured hot, dry, lazy, bringing with it, perhaps, some quiet feeling of content, unromantic and cheerful. The walls, the trees, the sanded walks, seemed to radiate back into the fair cloudless sky the sweltering late summer heat and yet they laughed and baked happily. The hour brought some odd sensition of comfort to the farmer in a nearby field, drying his brow for a moment by his thirsty horse, and to the lay-brother opening boxes behind the monastery kitchen.

The man walked up and down on the bank above the creek. He had been walking for half an hour. The lay-brother looked at him quizzically as he passed and murmured an invocation. It was always hard, this hour before taking first vows. Eighteen years before one, the world just behind. The lay-brother had seen many in this same situation, some white and nervous, some grim and determined, some despairing. Then, when the bell tolled five, there were the vows and usually the novice felt better. It was this hour in the country when the world seemed gloriously apparent and the monastery vaguely impotent. The lay-brother shook his head in sympathy and passed on.

The man's eyes were bent upon his prayer-book. He was very young, twenty at the most, and his dark hair in disorder gave him an even more boyish expression. A light flush lay on his calm face and his lips moved incessantly. He was not nervous. It seemed to

81

him as if he had always known he was to become a priest. Two
years before, he had felt the vague stirring, the transcendent sense
of seeing heaven in everything, that warned him softly, kindly that
the spring of his life was coming. He had given himself every
opportunity to resist. He had gone a year to college, four months
abroad, and both experiences only increased within him the
knowledge of his destiny. There was little hesitation. He had at
first feared self-committal with a thousand nameless terrors. He
thought he loved the world. Panicky, he struggled, but surer and
surer he felt that the last word had been said. He had his vocation—
and then, because he was no coward, he decided to become a
priest.

Through the long month of his probation he alternated between
deep, almost delirous, joy and the same vague terror at his own
love of life and his realization of all he sacrificed. As a favorite
child he had been reared in pride and confidence in his ability,
in faith in his destiny. Careers were open to him, pleasure, travel,
the law, the diplomatic service. When, three months before, he
had walked into the library at home and told his father that he
was going to become a Jesuit priest, there was a family scene and
letters on all sides from friends and relatives. They told him he was
ruining a promising young life because of a sentimental notion of
self sacrifice, a boyish dream. For a month he listened to the bitter
melodrama of the commonplace, finding his only rest in prayer,
knowing his salvation and trusting in it. After all, his worst battle
had been with himself. He grieved at his father's disappointment
and his mother's tears, but he knew that time would set them
right.

And now in half an hour he would take the vows which pledged
him forever to a life of service. Eighteen years of study—eighteen
years where his every thought, every idea would be dictated to him,
where his individuality, his physical ego would be effaced and he
would come forth strong and firm to work and work and work. He
felt strangely calm, happier in fact than he had been for days and
months. Something in the fierce, pulsing heat of the sun likened

itself to his own heart, strong in its decision, virile and doing its own share in the work, the greatest work. He was elated that he had been chosen, he from so many unquestionably singled out, unceasingly called for. And he had answered.

The words of the prayers seemed to run like a stream into his thoughts, lifting him up peacefully, serenely; and a smile lingered around his eyes. Everything seemed so easy; surely all life was a prayer. Up and down he walked. Then of a sudden something happened. Afterwards he could never describe it except by saying that some undercurrent had crept into his prayer, something unsought, alien. He read on for a moment and then it seemed to take the form of music. He raised his eyes with a start—far down the dusty road a group of negro hands were walking along singing, and the song was an old song that he knew:

> "We hope ter meet you in heavan whar we'll
> Part no mo',
> Whar we'll part no mo'.
> Gawd a'moughty bless you twel we
> Me-et again."

Something flashed into his mind that had not been there before. He felt a sort of resentment toward those who had burst in upon him at this time, not because they were simple and primitive, but because they had vaguely disturbed him. That song was old in his life. His nurse had hummed it through the dreamy days of his childhood. Often in the hot summer atfternoons he had played it softly on his banjo. It reminded him of so many things: months at the seashore on the hot beach with the gloomy ocean rolling around him, playing with sand castles with his cousin; summer evenings on the big lawn at home when he chased fireflys and the breeze carried the tune over the night to him from the negro-quarters. Later, with new words, it had served as a serenade—and now—well, he had done with that part of life, and yet he seemed to see a girl with kind eyes, old in a great sorrow, waiting, ever waiting. He seemed to hear voices calling, children's voices. Then around him swirled the city, busy with the hum of men; and there was a family that would never be, beckoning him.

Other music ran now as undercurrent to his thoughts: wild, incoherent, music, illusive and wailing, like the shriek of a hundred violins, yet clear and chord-like. Art, beauty, love and life passed in a panorama before him, exotic with the hot perfumes of world-passion. He saw struggles and wars, banners waving somewhere, voices giving hail to a king—and looking at him through it all were the sweet sad eyes of the girl who was now a woman.

Again the music changed; the air was low and sad. He seemed to front a howling crowd who accused him. The smoke rose again around the body of John Wycliffe, a monk knelt at a prie-dieu and laughed because the poor had not bread, Alexander VI pressed once more the poisoned ring into his brother's hand, and the black robed figures of the inquisition scowled and whispered. Three great men said there was no God, a million voices seemed to cry, "Why! Why! must we believe?" Then as in a chrystal he seemed to hear Huxley, Nietzsche, Zola, Kant cry, "I will not"—He saw Voltaire and Shaw wild with cold passion. The voices pleaded "Why?" and the girl's sad eyes gazed at him with infinite longing.

He was in a void above the world—the ensemble, everything called him now. He could not pray. Over and over again he said senselessly, meaninglessly, "God have mercy, God have mercy." For a minute, an eternity, he trembled in the void and then—something snapped. They were still there, but the girl's eyes were all wrong, the lines around her mouth were cold and chiselled and her passion seemed dead and earthy.

He prayed, and gradually the cloud grew clearer, the images appeared vague and shadowy. His heart seemed to stop for an instant and then—he was standing by the bank and a bell was tolling five. The reverend superior came down the steps and toward him.

"It is time to go in." The man turned instantly.

"Yes, Father, I am coming."

II.

The novices filed silently into the chapel and knelt in prayer. The blessed Sacrament in the gleaming monstrance was exposed among the flaming candles on the altar. The air was rich and heavy with incense. The man knelt with the others. A first chord of the magnificat, sung by the concealed choir above, startled him; he looked up. The late afternoon sun shone through the stained glass window of St. Francis Xavier on his left and fell in red tracery on the cassock of the man in front of him. Three ordained priests knelt on the altar. Above them a huge candle burned. He watched it abstractedly. To the right of him a novice was telling his beads with trembling fingers. The man looked at him. He was about twenty-six with fair hair and green-grey eyes that darted nervously around the chapel. They caught each other's eye and the elder glanced quickly at the altar candle as if to draw attention to it. The man followed his eye and as he looked he felt his scalp creep and tingle. The same unsummoned instinct filled him that had frightened him half an hour ago on the bank. His breath came quicker. How hot the chapel was. It was too hot; and the candle was wrong—wrong—everything suddenly blurred. The man on his left caught him.

"Hold up," he whispered, "they'll postpone you. Are you better? Can you go through with it?"

He nodded vaguely and turned to the candle. Yes, there was no mistake. Something was there, something played in the tiny flame, curled in the minute wreath of smoke. Some evil presence was in the chapel, on the very altar of God. He felt a chill creeping over him, though he knew the room was warm. His soul seemed paralyzed, but he kept his eyes riveted on the candle. He knew that he must watch it. There was no one else to do it. He must not take his eyes from it. The line of novices rose and he mechanically reached his feet.

"Per omnia saecula, saeculorum. Amen."

Then he felt suddenly that something corporeal was missing—his last earthly support. He realized what it was. The man on his left had gone out overwrought and shaken. Then it began. Something before had attacked the roots of his faith; had matched his world-sense against his God-sense, had brought, he had thought, every power to bear against him; but this was different. Nothing was denied, nothing was offered. It could best be described by saying that a great weight seemed to press down upon his innermost soul, a weight that had no essence, mental or physical. A whole spiritual realm evil in its every expression engulfed him. He could not think, he could not pray. As in a dream he heard the voices of the men beside him singing, but they were far away, farther away from him than anything had ever been before. He existed on a plane where there was no prayer, no grace; where he realized only that the forces around him were of hell and where the single candle contained the essence of evil. He felt himself alone pitted against an infinity of temptation. He could bring no parallel to it in his own experience or any other. One fact he knew: one man had succumbed to this weight and he must not—must not. He must look at the candle and look and look until the power that filled it and forced him into this plane died forever for him. It was now or not at all.

He seemed to have no body and even what he had thought was his innermost self was dead. It was something deeper that was he, something that he had never felt before. Then the forces gathered for one final attack. The way that the other novice had taken was open to him. He drew his breath quickly and waited and then the shock came. The eternity and infinity of all good seemed crushed, washed away in an eternity and infinity of evil. He seemed carried helplessly along, tossed this way and that—as in a black limitless ocean where there is no light and the waves grow larger and larger and the sky darker and darker. The waves were dashing him toward a chasm, a maelstrom everlastingly evil, and blindly, unseeingly, desperately he looked at the candle, looked at the flame which seemed like the one black star in the sky of despair. Then suddenly he became aware of a new presence. It seemed to come from the left, seemed consummated and expressed in warm, red tracery somewhere. Then he knew. It was the stained window of St. Francis Xavier. He gripped at it spiritually, clung to it and with aching heart called silently for God.

> *"Tantum ergo Sacramentum*
> *Veneremur cernui."*

The words of the hymn gathered strength like a triumphant paean of glory, the incense filled his brain, his very soul, a gate clanged somewhere and *the candle on the altar went out.*

"*Ego vos absolvo a peccatis tuis in nomine patris, filii, spiritus sancti.* Amen."

The file of novices started toward the altar. The stained lights from the windows mingled with the candle glow and the eucharist in its golden halo seemed to the man very mystical and sweet. It was very calm. The subdeacon held the book for him. He placed his right hand upon it.

"*In the name of the Father and the Son and of the Holy Ghost—*"

The Debutante

Many months after the publication of "The Ordeal," Miss Alida Bigelow of St. Paul received a letter which contained these remarks: "I'll send you a one-act play by me when it comes out in the next *Nassau Lit*. It's called 'The Debutante.'—It's a knockout!" (*The Letters of F. Scott Fitzgerald*, p. 450) No other apprentice work shows better form. Observing "Shadow Laurels'" precedent, "The Debutante" obeys the unities of time and place, the action taking about an hour and occurring in a boudoir. But to appreciate Fitzgerald's accomplishment here fully, one must have in mind the structural shortcomings of the other early writings.

The prep-school stories extend from about 800 words to about 3,000 words, their typical length being 2,000-2,500 words; and the college stories extend from about 2,000 words to about 5,700 words, their typical length being 3,500 words. Except in the one-act plays, where the unities are followed, increasingly complex structure accompanies the tendency toward greater bulk. While two of the seven prep-school stories have two parts, all six college stories have bi- and tri-partite constructions. Only rarely—as in "Pain and the Scientist," whose plot depends upon a reversal—do mechanical divisions provide organic support. Instead, they merely separate body and denouement or introduce a change of setting, both of which Fitzgerald managed in one-part stories. For instance, "The Trail of the Duke" (one part) treats a situation almost identical to that in "A Luckless Santa Claus" (two parts), and "The Mystery of the Raymond Mortgage" (one part) uses more settings than "The Room With the Green Blinds" (three parts). This unnecessarily elaborate and arbitrary structuring comes mainly from the stories' peripatetic quality. Some have dramatic beginnings and some surprise endings, but all have considerable movement.

It is no wonder, then, that Fitzgerald's first novel, *This Side of Paradise,* employs an elaborate mechanical organization: two Books separated by an Interlude, each containing several subdivided sections, which, though enabling the author to proceed scenically, make the construction episodic. Thus a work using consciously dramatic devices—scenes, one chapter a play, extensive dialogue—becomes, paradoxically enough, anything but dramatic. It is no wonder either that in *This Side of Paradise* many other places (Minneapolis, Lake Geneva, Connecticut, Maryland) appear with the main settings of Princeton and New York City. Only when Scott Fitzgerald's fiction fully assimilated the architectural skills he at least became aware of as a playwright did he manage to fashion formally sound stories and novels. The magnificently dramatic *Gatsby* is, of course, the best example.

Part of the power of "The Debutante," which, like "Babes in the Woods," takes the love-game for its central situation and the *femme fatale* for its central character, derives from Fitzgerald's frustrating courtship of Ginevra King. But neither this nor his bad grades nor his losing honors such as the presidency of the Triangle Club completely explains the burst of energy which culminated with the publication of five important works between January and June of 1917. Andrew Turnbull contends: "He had come to Princeton seeking a purchase for his talents and had tapped one avenue of advance after another, beginning with *The Tiger* and the Triangle. By degrees his center of gravity had shifted toward the *Lit,* for he had made up his mind to be a great writer, if not in a class with Shakespeare then in the class just below—with Keats, say, or Marlowe." (*Scott Fitzgerald,* p. 73)

The Smart Set would soon be publishing "Babes in the Woods" (September, 1919), "The Debutante" (November, 1919), and "Tarquin of Cheapside," correctly spelled (February, 1921). Versions of the first two, plus material from "The Spire and the

Gargoyle" and "Sentiment—and the Use of Rouge," would soon be appearing in *This Side of Paradise,* and not long after, "Tarquin of Cheapside" would be included in *Tales of the Jazz Age* (New York, 1922). According to Mr. Turnbull, "Fitzgerald would look back on this chaotic year [1916-1917] as the foundation of his literary life." (*Ibid.*)

The Debutante

The scene is a boudoir, or whatever you call a lady's room which hasn't a bed. Smaller rooms communicate with it, one on each side. There is a window at the left and a door leading into the hall at the back. A huge pier-glass stands in the corner; it is the only object in the room which is not littered with an infinitude of tulle, hat-boxes, empty boxes, full boxes, ribbons and strings, dresses, skirts, suits, lingerie, petticoats, lace, open jewel-cases, sashes, belts, stockings, slippers, shoes—perfectly littered with more than all this. In the very middle of the confusion stands a girl. She is the only thing in the room which looks complete, or nearly complete. She needs to have her belt hooked, and has too much powder on her nose; but aside from that, looks as though she might be presented to almost anything at almost any time; which is just what is going to happen to her. She is terrifically pleased with herself and the long mirror is the focus of her activity. Her rather discontented face is consciously flexible to the several different effects. Expression number one seems to be a simple, almost childish, ingenue, upward glance, concentrated in the eyes and the exquisitely angelic eyelashes. When expression number two is assumed, one forgets the eyes and the mouth is the center of the stage. The lips seem to turn from rose to a positive, unashamed crimson. They quiver slightly—where is the ingenue? Disappeared. Good evening Sapho, Venus, Madam Du—no! ah! Eve, simply Eve! The pier-glass seems to please. Expression number three:— Now her eyes and lips combine. Can this be the last stronghold? The aesthetic refuge of womanhood; her lips are drawn down at the corners, her eyes droop and almost fill with tears. Does her face turn paler? Does—No! Expression one has dismissed tears and pallor, and again—

HELEN—What time is it?

(The sewing machine stops in the room at the left.)

VOICE—I haven't a watch, Miss Helen.

HELEN—*(Assuming expression number three and singing to the mirror.)* "Poor butterfly—by the blossoms waiting—poor butter——" What time do you think it is, Narry, old lady? Where's mother, Narry?

NARRY—*(Rather crossly)* I am sure I haven't the slightest idea.

HELEN—Narry! *(No answer.)* Narry, I called you Old Lady, because—*(She pauses. The sewing machine swings into an emphatic march)* because it's the last chance I will have.

The machine stops again and Narry comes into the room sniffing. Narry is exactly of the mould with which the collective temperaments of Helen and her family have stamped her. She is absolutely adamant with everyone not a member of the family and absolutely putty in the hands of the least capable of them.

NARRY—You might just not call me Old Lady. *(She sniffs, and handkerchiefs herself)* Goodness gracious! I feel old enough now with you going out.

HELEN—Coming!

NARRY—Coming—

HELEN—*(Her mind wandering to her feet which carry her around the room to the sound of her voice)* "The moments pass into hours—the hours pass into years—and as she smiles through—"

Peremptory voice with the maternal rising accent ascends the stairs, and curls into the bedroom.

VOICE—Hel-*en.*

HELEN—*(With more volume than you would imagine could go with such a deliciously useless figure)* Yes, mother.

MOTHER—*(Drawing near.)* Are you very nearly ready, dear? . . I am coming up. I have had such a hard time with one of the waiters.

HELEN—I know mother, tight as he could be. Narry and I watched him try to get up when they threw him outside into the yard.

MOTHER—(*Now on the stairway landing*) You and Narry should not have done any such thing, Helen dear. I am surprised at Narry. I—(*She seems to pause and pant.*)

NARRY—(*Almost shouting*) I do declare, Mrs. Halycon. I——

Mrs. Halycon appears in the doorway and becomes the center of the stage. She is distinctly a factor in the family life. Neither her daughter's slang, nor her son's bills discourage her in the least. She is jeweled and rouged to the dowager point.

MRS. HALYCON—Now Narry, now Helen (*She produces a small notebook*) Sit down and be quiet (*Narry sits down anxiously on a chair which emerges from the screen of dresses. Helen returns to the pier-glass and the sequence of expressions passes over her face in regular rotation.*) Now I've made some notes here— let's see. I've made notes on things you must do. Just as I have thought of them, I have put them down. (*She seats herself somewhere and becomes severely judicial.*) First, and absolutely, you must not sit out with anyone. (*Helen looks bored.*) I've stood for it at your other dances and heaven knows how many dances of other people, but I will not, understand me, I will not endure to look all over for you when some friend of mine, or of your father's wants to meet you. You must tonight, you must all season —I mean you must stay in the ballroom, or some room where I can find you when I want you. Do you understand?

HELEN—(*Yawning*) Oh, yes! You would think I didn't know what to do.

MRS. HALYCON—Well, do it if you know how. I will not endure finding you in a dark corner of the conservatory, exchanging silliness with anyone, or listening to it.

HELEN—(*Sarcastically*) Yes, listening to it *is* better.

MRS. HALYCON—And you positively cannot give more than two dances to young Cannel. I will not have everyone in town having you engaged before you have had a fair chance.

HELEN—Same old line. You'd think from the way you talk that I was some horrible old man-chaser, or someone so weak and wobbly that you'd think I'd run off with someone. Mother, for heaven's sake—

Mrs. Halycon—My dear, I am doing my very best for you.

Helen—(*Wearily*) I know. (*She sits down decidedly on another invisible chair*) Mother, I happen, my dear, to have four dances with John Cannel. He called up, asked me for four of them, and what could I say? Besides, it's a cut-in-dance, and he would cut in as much as he wants anyhow. So what's the difference? (*Becoming impatient*) You can't run everything now, the way they did in the early nineties.

Mrs. Halycon—Helen, I've told you before that you can't say early nineties to me.

Helen—Don't treat me like a child then.

Mr. Halycon comes in. He is a small man with a large appearance and a board-of-directors heartiness.

Mr. Halycon—(*Feeling that the usual thing is expected of him*) Well, how is my little debutante daughter? About to flit into the wide, wide world?

Helen—No, daddy, just taking a more licensed view of it.

Mr. Halycon—(*Almost apologetically*) Helen, I want you to meet a particular friend of mine, a youngish man—

Helen—About forty-five?

Mrs. Halycon—Helen!

Helen—Oh, I like them forty-five. They know life, and are so adorably tired looking.

Mr. Halycon—And he is very anxious to meet you. He saw you when you came into my office one day, I believe—and let me tell you, he is a brainy man. Brought up from Providence by the——

Helen—(*Interrupting*) Yes, daddy, I'll be delighted to meet him. I'll——

Enter Cecilia, Helen's younger sister. Cecilia is sixteen, but socially precocious and outrageously wise on all matters pertaining to her sister. She has blonde hair, in contrast to her sister's dark brown; and besides, remarkable green eyes with a wistful trusting expression in them. However, there are very few people whom she trusts.

CECILIA—(*Calmly surveying the disorder around her*) Nice looking room.

HELEN—Well, what do you expect? Nothing but milliners, dressmakers and clumsy maids all day (*Narry rises and leaves the room*) What's the matter with her?

MRS. HALYCON—You've hurt her feelings.

HELEN—Have I? What time is it?

MRS. HALYCON—Quarter after eight. Are you ready? You've got too much powder on.

HELEN—I know it.

MR. HALYCON—Well, look me up when you come down; I want to see you before the rush. I'll be in the library with your uncle.

MRS. HALYCON—And don't forget the powder.

Mr. and Mrs. Halycon go out.

HELEN—Hook up my belt, will you, Cecilia?

CECILIA—Yes. (*She sets at it, Helen in the meanwhile regarding herself in the mirror*) What are you looking at yourself all the time for?

HELEN—(*Calmly*) Oh, just because I like myself.

CECILIA—I am all twittered! I feel as if I were coming out myself. It is rotten of them not to let me come to the dance.

HELEN—Why you've just only put your hair up. You'd look ridiculous.

CECILIA—(*Quietly*) I know where you keep your cigarettes and your little silver bottle.

HELEN—(*Starting so as to unloosen several hooks which Cecilia patiently does over again*) Why, you horrible child! Do you go prying around among all my things?

CECILIA—All right, tell mother.

HELEN—What do you do, just go through my drawers like a common little sneak-thief?

CECILIA—No, I don't. I wanted a handkerchief, and I went to looking and I couldn't help seeing them.

HELEN—That's what comes of letting you children fool around with no chaperons, read anything you want to, and dance until two every Saturday night all summer. If it comes to that, I'll tell something I saw that I didn't say anything about. Just before we came into town, that night you asked me if you could take Blaine MacDonough home in the electric, I happened to be passing at the end of the drive by the club, and I saw him kiss you.

CECILIA—(*Unmoved*) We were engaged.

HELEN—(*Frantically*) Engaged! You silly little fool! If any older people heard that you two were talking like that, you wouldn't be allowed to go with the rest of your crowd.

CECILIA—That's all right, but you know why you didn't tell, because what were *you* doing down there by the drive with John Cannel?

HELEN—Hush! You little devil.

CECILIA—All right. We'll call it square. I just started by wanting to tell you that Narry knows where those cigarettes are too.

HELEN—(*Losing her head*) You and Narry have probably been smoking them.

CECILIA—(*Amused*) Imagine Narry smoking.

HELEN—Well, *you* have been anyway.

CECILIA—You had better put them somewhere else.

HELEN—I'll put them where you can't find them, and if you weren't going back to school this week, I would go to mother and tell her the whole thing.

CECILIA—Oh, no you wouldn't. You wouldn't even do it for my good. You're too selfish.

Helen, still very superior, marches into the next room. Cecilia goes softly to the door, slams it without going out, and disappears behind the bureau. She emerges tip-toe, takes a cushion from an arm chair, and retires again to her refuge. Helen again reappears. Almost immediately a whistle sounds outside, twice repeated. She looks annoyed and goes to the window.

HELEN—John!

JOHN—(*From below*) Helen, can I see you a moment?

HELEN—No, indeed, there are people all over the house. Mother would think I had gone mad if she saw us talking out of the window.

JOHN—(*Hopefully*) I'll climb up.

HELEN—John, don't, you'll tear your dress clothes. (*He is evidently making good, as deduced from a few muttered fragments, barely audible*) Look out for the spike by the ledge. (*A moment later he appears in the window, a young man of twenty-two, good looking, but at present not particularly cheerful.*)

HELEN—(*Sitting down*) You simple boy! Do you want the family to kill me? Do you realize how conspicuous you are?

JOHN—(*Hopefully*) I'd better come in.

HELEN—No, you had better not. Mother may be up at any moment.

JOHN—Better turn out the lights. I make a good movie standing like this on this ledge.

(*Helen hesitates and then turns out all the lights except an electric lamp on the dresser.*)

HELEN—(*Assuming an effective pose in the arm chair*) What on earth do you want?

JOHN—I want you. I want to know that you are mine when I see you dancing around with this crowd tonight.

HELEN—Well, I am not. I belong to myself tonight, or rather to the crowd.

JOHN—You've been rotten to me this week.

HELEN—Have I?

JOHN—You're tired of me.

HELEN—No, not that. The family. (*They have evidently been over this ground before.*)

JOHN—It isn't the family, and you know it.

HELEN—Well, to tell the truth, it isn't exactly the family.

JOHN—I know it isn't. It's me—and you, and I'm getting desperate. You've got to do something one way or the other. We are engaged, or——

HELEN—Well, we are not engaged.

JOHN—Then what are we? What do you think about me, or do you think about me? You never tell me any more. We're drifting apart. Please Helen——!

HELEN—It's a funny business, John, just how I do feel.

JOHN—It isn't funny to me.

HELEN—No, I don't suppose it is. You know, if you just weren't so in love with me——

JOHN—(*Gloomily*) Well, I am.

HELEN—You see, there is no novelty in that. I always know just what you are going to say.

JOHN—I wish I did. When you first met me, you used to tell me that you loved to hear me talk, because you never knew what I was going to say.

HELEN—Well, I've found out. I like to run things, but it gets monotonous to always know that I am the key to the situation. If we are together, and I feel high, we enjoy ourselves. If I feel unhappy, then we don't; or anyways you don't. How you're feeling never has anything to do with it.

JOHN—Wouldn't it be that way with most couples?

HELEN—Oh, I suppose so, it would be if I were the girl.

JOHN—Well, what do you want?

HELEN—I want—Oh, I'll be frank for once. I like the feeling of going after them, I like the thrill when you meet them and notice that they've got black hair that's wavey, but awfully neat, or have dark lines under their eyes, and look charmingly dissipated, or have funny smiles, that come and go and leave you wondering whether they smiled at all. Then I like the way they begin to follow you with their eyes. They're interested. Good! Then I begin to place him. Try to get his type, find what he likes; right then the romance begins to lessen for me and increase for him. Then come a few long talks.

JOHN—(*Bitterly*) I remember.

HELEN—Then, John here's the worst of it. There's a point where everything changes.

JOHN—(*Mournfully interested*) What do you mean?

HELEN—Well, sometimes it's a kiss and sometimes it's long before anything like that. Now if it's a kiss, it can do one of three things.

JOHN—Three! It's done a thousand to me.

HELEN—It can make him get tired of you; but a clever girl

can avoid this. It's only the young ones and the heroines of magazine epigrams that are kissed and deserted. Then there's the second possibility. It can make you tired of him. This is usual. He immediately thinks of nothing but being alone with the girl, and she, rather touchy about the whole thing, gets snappy, and he's first love sick, then discouraged, and finally lost.

JOHN—(*More grimly*) Go on.

HELEN—Then the third state is where the kiss really means something, where the girl lets go of herself and the man is in deadly earnest.

JOHN—Then they're engaged?

HELEN—Exactly.

JOHN—Weren't we?

HELEN—(*Emphatically*) No, we distinctly were not. I knew what I was doing every blessed second, John Cannel.

JOHN—Very well, don't be angry. I feel mean enough already.

HELEN—(*Coldly*) Do you?

JOHN—Where do I come in? This is all a very clever system of yours, and you've played through it, you go along your way looking for another movie hero with black hair, or light hair, or red hair, and I am left with the same pair of eyes looking at me, the same lips moving in the same words to another poor fool, the next——

HELEN—For Heaven sakes don't cry!

JOHN—Oh, I don't give a damn what I do!

HELEN—(*Her eyes cast down to where her toe traces a pattern on the carpet*) You are very young. You would think from the way you talk that it was my fault, that I tried not to like you.

JOHN—Young! Oh, I'm in the discard, I know.

HELEN—Oh, you'll find someone else.

JOHN—I don't want anyone else.

HELEN—(*Scornfully*) You're making a perfect fool of yourself. (*There is a silence. She idly kicks the heel of her slipper against the rung of the chair.*)

JOHN—(*Slowly*) It's this damn Charlie Wordsworth.

HELEN—(*Raising her eyes quickly*) If you want to talk like that you'd better go. Please go now.

(*She rises. John watches her a moment and then admits his defeat.*)

JOHN—Helen, don't let's do like this. Let's be friends. Good God, I never thought I would have to ask you for just that.

(*She runs over and takes his hand, affecting a hopeful cheerfulness which immediately revolts him. He drops her hand and disappears from the window. She leans out and watches him.*)

HELEN—Watch for that spike. Oh, John, I warned you. You've torn your clothes.

JOHN—(*Drearily from below*) Yes, I've torn my clothes. I certainly play in wonderful luck. Such an effective exit.

HELEN—Are you coming to the dance?

JOHN—No, of course I am not. Do you think I'd come just to see you and Charlie——

HELEN—(*Gently*) Good-night, John.

She closes the window. Outside a clock strikes nine. The clatter of a few people on the stairway comes muffled through the door. She turns on the lights and going up to glass looks long and with an intense interest at herself. A powder puff comes into use for an instant. An errant wisp of hair is tucked into position, and a necklace from somewhere slides into place.

MRS. HALYCON—(*Outside*) Oh, Helen!

HELEN—Coming, mother.

She opens the top bureau drawer, takes out a silver cigarette case, and a miniature silver flask, and places them in a side drawer of the writing desk. Then she turns out all the lights and opens the door. The tuning of violins comes in nervous twangs and discords up the stairs. She turns once more and stands by the window. From below, there is a sudden burst of sound, as the orchestra swings into "Poor Butterfly." The violins and faint drums and a confused chord from a piano, the rich odor of powder, and new silk, a blend of laughters all surge together into the room. She dances toward the mirror, kisses the vague reflection of her face, and runs out the door.

Silence for a moment. Bundled figures pass along the hall, sillouhetted against the lighted door. The laughter heard from below becomes doubled and multiplied. Suddenly a moving blur takes shape behind the bureau. It resolves itself into a human figure, which arises, tip-toes over and shuts the door. It crosses the room, and the lights go on again. Cecilia looks about her, and with the light of definite purpose in her rich green eyes goes to the desk drawer, takes out the minature flask and the cigarette case. She lights a cigarette, and puffing and coughing walks to the pier-glass.

CECILIA—(*Addressing her future self*) Oh, yes! Really coming out is such a farce nowadays, y'know. We really play around so much before we are seventeen, that it's positive anticlimax. (*Shaking hands with a visionary middle-aged man of the world*) Yes, I b'lieve I've heard m' sister speak of you. Have a puff. They're very good. They're Coronas. You don't smoke? What a pity.

She crosses to the desk and picks up the flask. From downstairs the rain of clapping between encores rises. She raises the flask, uncorks it, smells it, tastes a little, and then drinks about the equivalent of two cock-tails. She replaces the flask, makes a wry face and as the music starts again she fox-trots slowly around the room, waving the cigarette with intense seriousness, and watching herself in the long mirror.

CURTAIN

The Spire and the Gargoyle

In a generation when public schooling was the accepted pattern of American life—particularly in the Middle West—Scott Fitzgerald was sent to private schools. His record at Newman was poor (C−), but even though he could not have scored much higher on the college entrance examinations and makeups, he managed to "bicker" his way past the Admissions Committee, explaining that it would be heartless to turn down a fellow celebrating his seventeenth birthday! At Princeton his academic average was normally in the fifth group—approximately D−. In his junior year he was dropped for poor scholarship, and while he was later readmitted, he never received a degree, in part, of course, because in 1917 he entered the army.

Fitzgerald never denied his poor academic record; yet, like many another unsuccessful college student, he sometimes tried to rationalize it. He said in one article that the reason he had failed algebra, trigonometry, geometry, and hygiene at Princeton was that he spent his freshman year writing an operetta for the Triangle Club. More than once he blamed his extracurricular activities in this organization, *The Nassau Literary Magazine*, and *The Tiger* for his academic record. When he should have been studying, he was trying to learn how to write. Reminiscing about his school days in St. Paul, Fitzgerald said: "I wrote all through every class in school in the back of my geography book and the first year Latin and on the margins of themes and declensions and mathematic problems." ("Who's Who: F. Scott Fitzgerald," *Saturday Evening Post*, September 18, 1920)

He sometimes tried to transfer the blame from himself to his

teachers. "Your teacher," he wrote to Miss Cornelia Vas, "is probably an ass—most of them are, I've found." (*The Letters of F.
Scott Fitzgerald*, p. 470) From grade school, where he was repri-
manded for correcting an error of his teacher's, to Princeton,
where "some of the professors who were teaching poetry really
hated it and didn't know what it was about" (*Ibid.*, p. 88), where
the English department had "an uncanny knack of making literature distasteful to young men" ("Princeton"), and where "no
one of my English professors . . . ever suggested to his class that
books were being written in America" (Review of *Brass*, by
Charles Norris, *The Bookman*, November, 1921), Fitzgerald felt
that he had unfortunate experiences with teachers.

Rationalize his academic failure as he might, he frequently regretted his lost years in Academe. He wrote to his daughter:
"One time in sophomore year at Princeton, Dean West got up and
rolled out the great lines of Horace: 'Integer Vitae, scelerisque
pueris/Non eget mauris, facule nec arcu—' * —And I knew in
my heart that I had missed something by being a poor Latin
scholar, like a blessed evening with a lovely girl. It was a great
human experience I had rejected through laziness, through having
sown no painful seed." (*The Letters of F. Scott Fitzgerald*, p. 22)
This regret runs through the numerous reading lists he sent to his
daughter at Vassar and the "College of One" he created for Miss
Sheilah Graham.

Whatever the results shown in the classroom, Scott Fitzgerald
was reading during his Princeton days. John Peale Bishop, who
"made me see, in the course of a couple of months, the difference between poetry and non-poetry" (*Scott Fitzgerald*, p. 71),
remembered a conversation he and Fitzgerald had had shortly
after they arrived as freshmen. "We talked of books," Bishop
wrote, "those I had read, which were not many, those Fitzgerald
had read, which were even less, those he said he had read, which

* The lines should read:
>   "Integer vitae, scelerisque purus,
>   Non eget Mauris jaculis
>   Fusce, neque arcu, nec . . ."

were many, many more." (Alfred Kazin [ed.], *F. Scott Fitz-gerald: The Man and His Work*, Cleveland and New York, 1951, p. 46) But as time went on, Fitzgerald began to make up, in reading at least, for the time he had wasted in prep-school. He said in an undated, unaddressed letter: "It is the last two years in college that count. I got nothing out of my first two years—in the last I got my passionate love for poetry and historical perspec-tive and ideas in general (however superficially), that carried me full swing into my career." (The F. Scott Fitzgerald Papers)

His reading, though fairly wide, would be quite selective. He would pick the periods, the artists, and the genres congenial to his own particular talent—the lyric poetry of the English Renais-sance (Shakespeare); the early nineteenth century (Romantic poets, especially Keats); the late nineteenth century (French Sym-bolists, Browning, Swinburne, Kipling); the twentieth century (Brooke, Eliot); the novel of social realism (Thackeray, Butler, Norris, Dreiser, Proust, Wharton); the "novel of selection" (Flau-bert, James, Conrad, Joyce, Cather, Hemingway). When he out-grew certain writers, for example Wilde, Wells and Mackenzie, he would find new, more helpful models.

As Lionel Trilling, who heard in Scott Fitzgerald's prose a "con-nection with tradition and with mind," has contended, "It is hard to overestimate the benefit which came . . . from his having con-sciously placed himself in the line of the great." Surely, he took thought, "which, for a writer, means really knowing what his predecessors have done." Surely, he had "intellectual courage," a "grasp . . . of the traditional resources available to him." (*The Liberal Imagination*, New York, 1953, pp. 235-44)

The Spire and the Gargoyle

I

The night mist fell. From beyond the moon it rolled, clustered about the spires and towers, and then settled below them so that the dreaming peaks seemed still in lofty aspiration toward the stars. Figures that dotted the daytime like ants now brushed along as ghosts in and out of the night. Even the buildings seemed infinitely more mysterious as they loomed suddenly out of the darkness, outlined each by a hundred faint squares of yellow light. Indefinitely from somewhere a bell boomed the quarter hour and one of the squares of light in an east campus recitation hall was blotted out for an instant as a figure emerged. It paused and resolved itself into a boy who stretched his arms wearily, and advancing threw himself down full length on the damp grass by the sun-dial. The cool bathed his eyes and helped to force away the tiresome picture of what he had just left, a picture that, in the two strenuous weeks of examinations now just over, had become indelibly impressed upon his memory—a room with the air fairly vibrating with nervous tension, silent with presence of twenty boys working desperately against time, searching every corner of tired brains for words and figures which seemed forever lost. The boy out on the grass opened his eyes and looked back at the three pale blurs which marked the windows of the examination room. Again he heard:

"There will be fifteen minutes more allowed for this examination." There had followed silence broken by the snapping of verifying watches and the sharp frantic race of pencils. One by one the seats had been left vacant and the little preceptor with the tired look had piled the booklets higher. Then the boy had left the room to the music of three last scratching pencils.

In his case it all depended on this examination. If he passed it he would become a sophomore the following fall; if he failed, it meant that his college days faded out with the last splendors of June. Fifty cut recitations in his first wild term had made necessary the extra course of which he had just taken the examination. Winter muses, unacademic and cloistered by Forty-second Street and Broadway, had stolen hours from the dreary stretches of February and March. Later, time had crept insidiously through the lazy April afternoons and seemed so intangible in the long Spring twilights. So June found him unprepared. Evening after evening the senior singing, drifting over the campus and up to his window, drew his mind for an instant to the unconscious poetry of it and he, goading on his spoiled and over-indulged faculties, bent to the revengeful books again. Through the careless shell that covered his undergraduate consciousness had broken a deep and almost reverent liking for the gray walls and gothic peaks and all they symbolized in the store of the ages of antiquity.

In view of his window a tower sprang upward, grew into a spire, yearning higher till its uppermost end was half invisible against the morning skies. The transiency and relative unimportance of the campus figures except as holders of a sort of apostolic succession had first impressed themselves on him in contrast with this spire. In a lecture or in an article or in conversation, he had learned that Gothic architecture with its upward trend was peculiarly adapted to colleges, and the symbolism of this idea had become personal to him. Once he had associated the beauty of the campus night with the parades and singing crowds that streamed through it, but in the last month the more silent stretches of sward and the quiet halls with an occasional late-burning scholastic light held his imagination with a stronger grasp— and this tower in full view of his window became the symbol of his perception. There was something terribly pure in the slope of the chaste stone, something which led and directed and called.

To him the spire became an ideal. He had suddenly begun trying desperately to stay in college.

"Well, it's over," he whispered aloud to himself, wetting his hands in the damp, and running them through his hair. "All over."

He felt an enormous sense of relief. The last pledge had been duly indited in the last book, and his destiny lay no longer in his own hands, but in those of the little preceptor, whoever he was: the boy had never seen him before—and the face,—he looked like one of the gargoyles that nested in dozens of niches in some of the buildings. His glasses, his eyes, or his mouth gave a certain grotesque upward slant to his whole cast of feature, that branded him as of gargoyle origin, or at least gargoyle kinship. He was probably marking the papers. Perhaps, mused the boy, a bit of an interview, an arrangement for a rereading in case of the ever possible failure would be—to interrupt his thought the light went out in the examination room and a moment later three figures edged along the path beside him while a fourth struck off south towards the town. The boy jumped to his feet and, shaking himself like a wet spaniel, started after the preceptor. The man turned to him sharply as he murmured a good evening and started trudging along beside.

"Awful night," said the boy.

The gargoyle only grunted.

"Gosh, that was a terrible examination." This topic died as unfruitfully as that of the weather, so he decided to come directly to the point.

"Are you marking these papers, sir?"

The preceptor stopped and faced him. Perhaps he didn't want to be reminded of the papers, perhaps he was in the habit of being exasperated by anything of this sort, but most probably he was tired and damp and wanted to get home.

"This isn't doing you any good. I know what you're going to say—that this is the crucial examination for you and that you'ld like me to go over your paper with you, and so on. I've heard the same thing a hundred times from a hundred students in the course of this last two weeks. My answer is 'No, No,' do you understand? I don't care to know your identity and I won't be followed home by a nagging boy."

Simultaneously each turned and walked quickly away, and the boy suddenly realized with an instinct as certain as divination that he was not going to pass the examination.

"Damned gargoyle," he muttered.

But he knew that the gargoyle had nothing to do with it.

II

Regularly every two weeks he had been drifting out Fifth Avenue. On crisp autumn afternoons the tops of the shining auto busses were particularly alluring. From the roofs of other passing busses a face barely seen, an interested glance, a flash of color assumed the proportion of an intrigue. He had left college five years before and the busses and the art gallery and a few books were his intellectual relaxation. Freshman year Carlisle's "Heroes and Hero-Worship," in the hands of an impassioned young instructor had interested him particularly. He had read practically nothing. He had neither the leisure to browse thoughtfully on much nor the education to cram thoughtfully on little, so his philosophy of life was molded of two elements: one the skeptical office philosophy of his associates, with a girl, a ten thousand dollar position, and a Utopian flat in some transfigured Bronx at the end of it; and the other, the three or four big ideas which he found in the plain speaking Scotchman, Carlyle. But he felt, and truly, that his whole range was pitifully small. He was not naturally bookish; his taste could be stimulated as in the case of "Heroes and Hero-Worship" but he was still and now always would be in the stage where every work and very author had to be introduced and sometimes interpreted to him. "Sartor Resartus" meant nothing to him nor ever could.

So Fifth Avenue and the top of the busses had really grown to stand for a lot. They meant relief from the painted, pagan crowds of Broadway, the crowded atmosphere of the blue serge suits and grated windows that he met down town and the dingy middle class cloud that hovered on his boarding house. Fifth

Avenue had a certain respectability which he would have once despised; the people on the busses looked better fed, their mouths came together in better lines. Always a symbolist, and an idealist, whether his model had been a profligate but magnetic sophomore or a Carlylized Napoleon, he sought around him in his common life for something to cling to, to stand for what religions and families and philosophies of life had stood for. He had certain sense of fitness which convinced him that his old epicureanism, romantic as it might have been in the youth of his year at college, would have been exotic and rather disgusting in the city itself. It was much too easy; it lacked the penance of the five o'clock morning train back to college that had faced himself and his fellow student revelers, it lacked the penance of the long morning in classes, and the poverty of weeks. It had been something to have a reputation, even such a reputation as this crowd had had, but dissipation from the New York standpoint seemed a matter of spats and disgustingly rich Hebrews, and shoddy Bohemeanism had no attraction for him.

Yet he was happy this afternoon. Perhaps because the bus on which he rode was resplendent in its shining new coat of green paint, and the stick-of-candy glamor of it had gone into his disposition. He lit a cigarette and made himself rather comfortable until he arrived at his destination. There were only certain sections of the museum that he visited. Statuary never attracted him, and the Italian madonnas and Dutch gentlemen with inconsequent gloves and books in the foreground rather bored him. It was only here and there in an old picture tucked away in the corner that his eye caught the glare of light on snow in a simple landscape or the bright colors and multiple figures of a battle painting, and he was drawn into long and detailed fits of contemplation and frequent revisits.

On this particular afternoon he was wandering rather aimlessly from one room to another when he suddenly noticed a small man in overshoes, his face latticed with enormous spectacles, thumbing a catalogue in front of a Flemish group. He started, and with a sense of recollection walked by him several times. Suddenly he realized that here was that one time instrument of his fate, the gargoyle, the little preceptor who had flunked him in his crucial examination.

Oddly enough his first sensation was one of pleased reminiscence and a desire for conversation. Following that he had a curious feeling of shyness, untinged by any bitterness. He paused, staring heavily, and instantly the huge glasses glimmered suspiciously in his eyes.

"Pardon me sir, but do you remember me?" he asked eagerly.

The preceptor blinked feverishly.

"Ah——no."

He mentioned the college and the blinks became more optimistic. He wisely decided to let the connection rest there The preceptor couldn't, couldn't possibly remember all the men who had passed before his two "Mirrors of Shallot" so why bring up old, accusing facts—besides—he felt a great desire to chat.

"Yes—no doubt—your face is familiar, you'll pardon my—my chilliness a moment since—a public place." He looked around depreciatingly. "You see, I've left the university myself."

"So you've gone up in the game?" He instantly regretted this remark for the little man answered rather quickly:

"I'm teaching in a high school in Brooklyn." Rather embarassed, the younger man tried to change the subject by looking at the painting before them, but the gargoyle grimly continued:

"I have—a—rather a large family, and much as I regretted leaving the University, the salary was unfortunately very much of a factor."

There was a pause during which both regarded the picture steadily. Then the gargoyle asked a question:

"How long since you've graduated?"

"Oh, I never graduated. I was there for only a short while." He was sure now that the gargoyle had not the slightest conception of his identity; he might rather enjoy this, however, and he had a pleasant notion that the other was not averse to his company.

"Are you staying here much longer?" The gargoyle was not,

and together they moved to a restaurant two blocks down where they indulged in milk, tea and jam and discussed the university. When six o'clock pushed itself into the crowded hours it was with real regret that they shook hands, and the little man, manipulating his short legs in mad expostulation, raced after a Brooklyn car. Yes, it had been distinctly exhilarating. They had talked of academic atmospheres, of hopes that lay in the ivied walls, of little things that could only have counted after the mystic hand of the separation had made them akin. The gargoyle had touched lightly upon his own story, of the work he was doing, of his own tepid, stuffy environment. It was his hope some day to get back, but now there were young appetites to satisfy (the other thought grotesquely of the young gargoyles)—if he could see his way clear in the next few years,—so it went, but through all his hopeful talk there was a kind of inevitability that he would teach in a Brooklyn high school till the last bell called him to his last class. Yes, he went back occasionally. He had a younger brother who was an instructor there.

So they had talked, knit together by the toast and the sense of exile. That night the shrivelled spinster on his left at table asked him what college he thought would be worthy of ushering her promising nephew into the outer world. He became voluble and discoursive. He spoke of ties that bind, of old associations, and remarked carelessly as he left her, that he was running back himself for a day the next week. But afterwards he lay awake and thought until the chairs and bedposts of his room became grey ghosts in the dawn.

III

The car was hot and stuffy with most of the smells of the state's alien population. The red plush seats radiated dust in layers and stratas. The smoking car had been even more impossible with filthy floor and heavy air. So the man sat next to a partly open window in the coach and shivered against the cutting cloud of fog that streamed in over him. Lights sped by vaguely blurred and spreading, marking towns and farmhouses with the demo-

cratic indiscrimination of the mist. As the conductor heralded
each station the man felt a certain thrill at the familiarity of the
names. The times and conditions under which he had heard them
revolved in a medley of memories of his one year. One station
particularly near the university had a peculiar significance for
him because of the different ways it had affected him while he
had been in college. He had noted it at the time. September of
his entrance year, it had been the point where he grew acutely
nervous and figidity. Returning that November from a foot ball
defeat, it had stood for all that seemed gloomy in the gloomy
college he was then going back to. In February it had meant the
place to wake and pull one's self together, and as he had passed
it for the last time that June, he had wondered with a sudden
sinking of his heart if it was to be the last time. Now as the train
shook and trembled there for a moment, he stared out the window, and tried to get an impression. Oddly enough his first one
came back to him; he felt rather nervous and uncertain.

He had discovered a few minutes ago that the little preceptor
sat ahead of him three seats, but the younger man had not joined
him or even addressed him. He wanted to draw to himself every
impression he could from this ride.

They drew in. Grip in hand, he swung off the train, and from
force of habit turned toward the broad steps that led to the
campus. Then he stopped and dropping his suit case, looked before him. The night was typical of the place. It was very like the
night on which he had taken his last examination, yet somehow
less full and less poignant. Inevitability became a reality and assumed an atmosphere of compelling and wearing down. Where
before the spirit of spires and towers had thrilled him and had
made him dreamily content and acquiescent, it now overawed
him. Where before he had realized only his own inconsequence,
he now realized his own impotence and insufficiency. The towers
in faint outlines and the battlemented walls of vague buildings
fronted him. The engine from the train he had just left wheezed
and clanged and backed; a hack drove off; a few pale self-effacing
town boys strode away voicelessly, swallowed up in the night.

And in front of him the college dreamed on—awake. He felt a nervous excitement that might have been the very throb of its slow heart.

A figure brushed violently into him, almost knocking him off his feet. He turned and his eyes pierced the trembling darkness of the arclight to find the little preceptor blinking apprehensively at him from his gargoyle's eyes.

"Good evening."

He was hesitatingly recognized.

"Ah—how do you do? How do you do? Foggy evening, hope I didn't jar you."

"Not at all. I was just admiring the serenity." He paused and almost felt presumptuous.

"Are you—ah—pretending to be a student again?"

"I just ran out to see the place. Stay a night perhaps." Somehow this sounded far-fetched to him. He wondered if it did to the other.

"Yes?—I'm doing the same thing. My brother is an instructor here now you know. He's putting me up for a space." For an instant the other longed fiercely that he too might be invited to be "put up for a space."

"Are you walking up my way?"

"No—not quite yet."

The gargoyle smiled awkwardly. "Well, good-night." There was nothing more to say. Eyes staring, he watched the little figure walking off, propelled jerkily by his ridiculous legs.

Minutes passed. The train was silent. The several blurs on the station platform became impersonal and melted into the background. He was alone face to face with the spirit that should have dominated his life, the mother that he had renounced. It was a stream where he had once thrown a stone but the faint ripple had long since vanished. Here he had taken nothing, he had given nothing; nothing?—his eyes wandered slowly upward—up—up—until by straining them he could see where the spire began—and with his eyes went his soul. But the mist was upon both. He could not climb with the spire.

A belated freshman, his slicker rasping loudly, slushed along the soft path. A voice from somewhere called the inevitable formula toward an unknown window. A hundred little sounds of the current drifting on under the fog pressed in finally on his consciousness.

"Oh God!" he cried suddenly, and started at the sound of his own voice in the stillness. He had cried out from a complete overwhelming sense of failure. He realized how outside of it all he was. The gargoyle, poor tired little hack, was bound up in the fabric of the whole system much more than he was or ever could be. Hot tears of anger and helplessness rushed to his eyes. He felt no injustice, only a deep mute longing. The very words that would have purged his soul were waiting him in the depths of the unknown before him—waiting for him where he could never come to claim them. About him the rain dripped on. A minute longer he stood without moving, his head bent dejectedly, his hands clenched. Then he turned, and picking up his suit case walked over to the train. The engine gave a tentative pant, and the conductor, dozing in a corner, nodded sleepily at him from the end of the deserted car. Wearily he sank onto a red plush seat, and pressed his hot forehead against the damp window pane.

Tarquin of Cheepside

Scott Fitzgerald's partiality for "Tarquin of Cheepside," which, characteristically, he misspelled, is attested to both by his Princeton contemporaries and his determination to include it in *Tales of the Jazz Age* (pp. 225-33) over the objections of his editor, Maxwell Perkins, who felt that people would resent the identity of the criminal and who found the narrative inadequate to the surprise ending. A historical fantasy like "The Room with the Green Blinds," "Tarquin" speculates about the autobiographical circumstances behind the composition of "The Rape of Lucrece." "The Spire and the Gargoyle" had suffered from personal involvement: whereas the apprentice fiction usually "shows," implies, there he had "told," made everything explicit. But "Tarquin" suffers from the opposite fault. It contends that the artist relies upon, even manufactures, experience for his subject matter, yet nothing could have been further from Fitzgerald than Shakespeare raping Lucrece's "real-life" model.

At the end of a review of Shane Leslie's *Verses in Peace and War*, which *The Nassau Literary Magazine* published two months after the story, Fitzgerald said: "Despite Mr. Taine, in the whole range from Homer's Oddysey to Master's idiocy, there has been but one Shakespeare." Fitzgerald was probably more interested in the great poet's songs and sonnets than in the plays, for among the volumes he would give to Miss Graham only *King Lear* is heavily marked, while five sonnets and twelve songs have been checked. He was or would become familiar with the work of Chaucer, Wyatt, Spenser (*The Faerie Queene*), Sidney, Lodge, Drayton, Marlowe, Dekker, Donne, Jonson, Herrick, Waller, Milton (*Paradise Lost*, "L'Allegro"), Suckling, Crashaw, and Marvell ("To His Coy Mistress").

Scott Fitzgerald was drawn to the lyrical aspect of English Renaissance literature, just as he was drawn to the works of the Romantics and neo-Romantics. This is consistent with his love for "pure poetry" in general, a lifelong affinity that unquestionably affected his prose style. He wrote to his daughter in July of 1940: "The chief fault in your style is its lack of distinction— something which is inclined to grow with the years. You had distinction once—there's some in your diary—and the only way to increase it is to cultivate *your own garden*. And the only thing that will help you is poetry which is the most concentrated form of style." (*The Letters of F. Scott Fitzgerald*, p. 86)

In the previously quoted *Saturday Evening Post* article of September 18, 1920, Fitzgerald had said: "The next year, 1916-17, found me back in college, but by this time I had decided that poetry was the only thing worthwhile, so with my head ringing with the meters of Swinburne and the matters of Rupert Brooke I spent the spring doing sonnets, ballads and rondels into the small hours." Whether or not they are influenced specifically by Swinburne or Brooke, all the *Nassau Lit* poems except the satiric "To My Unused Greek Book," which, nevertheless, borrows the ababcdedce pattern of "Ode on a Grecian Urn," are romantic lyrics. "Rain Before Dawn" is an impressionistic treatment of death; "Princeton—the Last Day" is about the transitoriness of time; "On a Play Twice Seen" is about lost love; "The Cameo Frame" is about the relation between art and life; "City Dusk" is about loneliness; "My First Love" is about illusion; "Marching Streets" is another impressionistic treatment of death, and "The Pope at Confession" is about the frailty of men.

Since the *femme fatale* represents the single romantic theme persistently conveyed by the essentially non-poetic prose and dialogue of the apprentice fiction and drama while most of the juvenile poems manifest a variety of such themes, it would seem that poetry had a conceptual as well as verbal impact on Fitzgerald's mature work. At any rate, with various modifications, additions, and changes of emphases, he was to take over much of the aesthetic of the Romantic poets: the use of the artist's personal experience as subject matter; the stress on the individual and his private world; the conflict between the world as it is and as it might be; the importance of heroic striving; the importance of the moment; the importance of wonder (man's capacity to respond to the infinite possibilities of his existence).

"Princeton—the Last Day" appeared in *The Nassau Literary Magazine* of May, 1917:

> The last light wanes and drifts across the land,
> The low, long land, the sunny land of spires.
> The ghosts of evening tune again their lyres
> And wander singing, in a plaintive band
> Down the long corridors of trees. Pale fires
> Echo the night from tower top to tower.
> Oh sleep that dreams and dream that never tires,
> Press from the petals of the lotus-flower
> Something of this to keep, the essence of an hour!
>
> No more to wait the twilight of the moon
> In this sequestrated vale of star and spire;
> For one, eternal morning of desire
> Passes to time and earthy afternoon.
> Here, Heracletus, did you build of fire
> And changing stuffs your prophecy far hurled
> Down the dead years; this midnight I aspire
> To see, mirrored among the embers, curled
> In flame, the splendor and the sadness of the world.

Tarquin of Cheepside

Running footsteps.—Light, soft-soled shoes, made of queer leathery cloth brought from Ceylon, setting the pace; thick flowing boots, two pairs, dark blue and gilt, reflecting the moonlight in blunt gleams and flashes, following, a hundred yards behind. Soft Shoes cleaves the moonlight for a haggard second, then darts into a blind labyrinth of alleys and becomes merely an unsteady scuffle in the darkness ahead. In go Flowing Boots with swords lurching and with clumsy stumbling, cursing the black lanes of London. Soft Shoes leaps a gate and straggles through a hedge-row. Flowing Boots leaps the gate and straggle through a hedge-row;—and there is the watch ahead—two murderous pikemen with ferocious expressions acquired in Calais and the Spanish marshes. But there is no cry for help. The pursued does not fall panting and clutching his purse at their feet nor do the pursuers raise a hue and cry— Soft Shoes goes by like a rush of air. The watch curse and hesitate, look behind and then spread their pikes grimly across the road and wait. A cloud scurries across the sky and blackens the narrow street.

Again the pale sheen skims the eaves and roofs; the chase is on once more, but one of Flowing Boots leaves a little black trail until he binds himself clumsily as he runs, with fine lace caught from his throat.

It was no case for the watch tonight. There had been devil's work and the devil seemed to be he who appeared faintly in front, heel over gate, knee over fence. Moreover, the adversary was evidently travelling near home, or in any rate, in that part of London consecrated to him, for the streets were narrowing and the houses hung over more and more, furnishing natural ambushes often utilized for battle, murder and sudden death. So they twisted, down long sinuous lanes where the moonlight was shut away, except for tiny patches and glints. Ahead the quarry was running blindly, minus his leather jerkin, dripping with sweat and scanning his ground carefully on both sides. Suddenly he slowed down and retracing his steps, darted down an alley darker and narrower and longer than any he had yet explored. Two hundred yards down he stopped short and crammed himself into a nitch in the wall where he huddled and panted silently like a grotesque god, very faintly outlined in the gloom.

Twenty yards beyond him the others stopped and he heard a whispered colloquy.

"Within thirty yards now."

"Yes, I was atune to that scuffle; it stopped!"

"He's hid."

"Stay together and, by the Virgin, we'll split him!"

Their voices lowered and Soft Shoes could hear no more, nor did he wait to, for at a stealthy step in his direction, he sprang in three paces across the alley, where he bounded up, flapped for a moment on the edge of the wall like a huge bird, and disappeared, gulped down by the hungry night at a mouthful.

   *   *   *   *   *   *   *   *   *   *

Peter Caxter read late, too late, he had recently discovered. His eyes were getting particularly dim for his young time of life, his stomach was swelling to portliness. Tall and misbuilt, lazy too, he was spurred on in his studies by conscience got in heartfuls at Cambridge, and ambition carefully distilled through her subjects by Elizabeth, by the grace of Luther, Queen of England. Peter having completed a rather painful sea-voyage, and stored up great hunks of Elizabethan anecdote for his future grandchildren, was now flitting cumberously back to his neglected books—and what a book he had this night! *The Faery Queene*, by one Edmund Spencer, lay before him under the wavering candle light.

"The Legend of Britomartis or of Chastity
It palls * me here to write of Chastity
The fayrest vertue, far above the rest"—

A sudden rush of feet on the stairs, and a man darted into the room, a man panting and gasping and on the verge of a collapse.

"Peter," he blurted out, "I must be hidden—I'm in a scrape—it's death if the two men who will come here after me find me!"

Peter showed little surprise. His guest had been in various difficulties before and had entrusted him with his extrication. And the visitor, when his gasps gave way to quick precise breathing, lost his culprit's air and looked very much at his ease. Indeed a casual observer might have said that he was proud of some recent exploit.

"Two fools with long swords and short wits harrying me over half of London like a terrified rabbit!"

"There were three fools in the chase then," said Peter ironicly, as he took a pole from a corner and dislodged a trap door which led to a sort of garret above. He pointed upward. The other crouched, jumped, caught at the edge of the aperture and, struggling for a moment, swung himself up and was lost in the darkness above. The hatch was replaced, there was a scurry like the exodus of rats, an oath muffled by the floor, then silence. Peter picked up the "Legend of Britomartis or of Chastity" and settling himself—waited.

Five minutes later a scramble on the stairs was followed by a prolonged hammering on the door. He sighed, put down the book, and picking up the candle, rose.

"Who is there?"

"Open—Or we will burst in the door!"

Peter opened it a bare eight inches and held the candle high. He pitched his voice so that it sounded timorous and querulous.

"May not a peaceable citizen of London rest undisturbed from marauders for one small hour of the night?"

* I.e., falls.

"Open gossip, and quick, or we'll pitch a yard of steel through the crack there!"

The shadows of the two gallants fell in huge wavering outlines over the moonlit stairs, and by the light Peter characterized his opponents in a quick glance. They were gentlemen, hastily but richly attired. One was a man of thirty, greatly distraught and nervous from intense excitement and anxiety. The other, the one with the bloody hand, was younger, and though he was quiet and restrained, his lips were set with grim purpose. Peter let them in.

"Is there a man hidden here?" said the elder fiercely.

"No."

"Has there been anyone on the stairs?"

Peter replied that ten minutes ago there had been some one on the landing below trying to get into a room, but that whoever he had been, he had failed and gone away. Would they be so kind as to inform him for whom they were searching and why.

"There has been violence done—to a woman," said the younger man slowly. "My sister—and his wife. Who we are does not matter. If you are hiding this man it may cost you your life."

"Do you know who he—this man—is?" asked Peter quickly.

The elder man sank onto a chair and dropped his face in his hands.

"God's Word—We do not know even that."

Peter rather winced. This was more tragedy than he had bargained for.

The younger man had been searching about Peter's two rooms, poking his sword into anything that looked at all suspicious. He noticed the trap door.

"What's that?"

"It is not used," said Peter. "It is an attic—the trap is nailed down." Suddenly he thought of the pole and drew in his breath sharply, but the other turned away with an air of finality.

"It would take ten minutes to get up there without a ladder unless the man were a tumbler."

"A tumbler," repeated the elder dully.

"Let us go."

They went silently, sad and impotent, and Peter closed and
barred the door after them. After a safe ten minutes he took the
pole and poked the trap door open. When the other stood before
him he began:

"There has been deviltry in your life, and much of it—there
have been drinking and women and blood, but when I face two
men with a tale even half told like this——."

His guest stopped him.

"Peter—you'd never understand. You've helped me before.
You've got to, got to help me now. Do you hear? I shall not argue.
I want pen and paper and your bedroom, Peter." He grew angry.
"Peter are you trying to interfere—what right have you? I am re-
sponsible only to myself for what I do."

He took a pen and ink and a sheaf of paper from the table
and without another word walked into the other room and
shut the door. Peter grunted, started after him and then recon-
sidering, went back and picking up *The Faery Queene* sank into
his chair.

Three o'clock went into four. The room paled and the dark
outside became damp and chill—and Peter bent low over his table,
tracing through the pattern of *The Faery Queene*. Dragons
chortled along the narrow streets outside; when the sleepy ar-
mourer's boy began his work at five, the heavy clink and clank
of plate and linked mail swelled to the significance of marching cavalcades.

The fog shut down at the first streak of dawn and the room
was greyish yellow at six when Peter tiptoed to his cupboard bedroom and opened the door. His guest turned to him red-eyed,
death-pale, unseeing. He had been writing hard and the Prie-dieu
on which he wrote was piled with a stack of paper, while around
on the floor were littered scraps of almost virgin pages. Peter
softly closed the door and returned to his syren. Outside, the
clump of boots, the croaking of old beldames from attic to attic,
the dull murmur of morning, unnerved him, and, half dozing he
slumped in his chair and his dreaming brain worked chaoticaly
on the imagery that stacked it. He was on a cloud and the way

to heaven lay over groaning bodies crushed near the sun. He shuddered and tread the way. He was in a wood where he killed a bird of paradise for its plumage. Some one was trying to barter his soul for the world, and the soul was bartered. When a hot hand touched his shoulder he awoke with a start. The fog was thick in the room and his guest seemed a grey ghost, made of some like misty stuff, where he stood beside him, the sheaf of paper in his hand.

"Read this, Peter, and lock. it away and let me sleep until to-morrow."

Peter took the pile and looked at it curiously. The other threw himself down full length on the couch and sank almost immediately into a deep slumber, with breathing regular, but brow wrinkled in queer corners.

Peter yawned sleepily and glanced at the scrawled first page—then he began reading aloud softly:

The Rape of Lucrece.
"From the beseiged Ardea all in post,
Borne by the trustless wings of false desire,
Lust-breathing Tarquin leaves the Roman host,——"

Babes in the Woods

The "Ledger" entry of July, 1901, reads, "His sister Annabel was born. His first certain memory is the sight of her howling on a bed." At five, Fitzgerald had, of course, no idea that "at 19 or so" he would be concerning himself with her conduct around boys. Andrew Turnbull has described the future situation: "Up till now Fitzgerald hadn't much to do with his sister . . . She was quiet and pretty, and he was proud of her and anxious that she make the most of her possibilities. To this end he wrote her lengthy instructions." (*Scott Fitzgerald*, p. 66)

Near the top of the initial page of these instructions the author later commented: "Basis of Bernice." This refers to "Bernice Bobs Her Hair," a story he placed in the *Saturday Evening Post* (May 1, 1920) and in *Flappers and Philosophers*. Marjorie, at whose home Bernice has been staying, explains the reasons her cousin is not more popular: "First, you have no ease of manner. Why? Because you're never sure about your personal appearance. When a girl feels that she's perfectly groomed and dressed she can forget that part of her. That's charm. The more parts of yourself you can afford to forget the more charm you have."

The instructions, which are transcribed here in their entirety, apply equally to "Babes in the Woods," for Isabelle, who "had been sixteen years old for two months," is an old hand at the love-game.

The General Subject of Conversation

Conversation like grace is a cultivated art. Only to the very few does it come naturally. You are as you know, not a good conversationalist and you might very naturally ask, "What do boys like to talk about?"

(1) Boys like to talk about themselves—much more than girls. A girl once, named Helen Walcott, told me (and she was the most popular debutante in Washington one winter) that as soon as she got a man talking about himself she had him cinched and harnessed—they give themself away. Here are some leading questions for a girl to use.

 a) You dance so much better than you did last year.
 b) How about giving me that sporty necktie when you're thru with it.
 c) You've got the longest eyelashes! (This will embarrass him, but he likes it)
 d) I hear you've got a "line"!
 e) Well who's you're latest crush?

Avoid
 a) When do you go back to school?
 b) How long have you been home?
 c) Its warm or the orchestra's good or the floor's good.

Also avoid any talk about relations or mutual friends. Its a sure sign you're hard up for talk if you ask Jack Allen about Harriette or Tuby about Martha. Dont be afraid of slang—use it, but be careful to use the most modern and sportiest like "line", camafluage etc. Never talk to a boy about about his school or college unless he's done something special or unless he starts the subject. In a conversation its always good to start by talking about nothing —just some fresh camafluage; but start it yourself—never let the boy start it. *Dont talk about your school—no matter where you go.* Never sing no matter how big the chorus.

2.

As you get a little old you'll find that boys like to talk about such things as smoking and drinking. Always be very liberal—boys hate a prig—tell them you dont object to a girl smoking but dont like cigarettes yourself. Tell them you smoke only cigars—kid them!— When you're old still you want always to have a line on the latest books plays and music. More men like that than you can imagine.

In your conversation always affect a complete frankness but really be only as frank as you wish to be. Never try to give a boy the affect that you're popular—Ginevra always starts by saying she's a poor unpopular woman without any beaux. Always pay close attention to the man. Look at him in his eyes if possible. Never effect boredom. Its terribly hard to do it gracefully Learn to be worldly. Remember in all society nine girls out of ten marry for money and nine men out of ten are fools.

Poise: Carriage: Dancing: Expression

(1) Poise depends on carriage, expression and conversation and having discussed the last and most important I'll say a few words on the other two.

(2) A girl should hold herself straight. Margaret Armstrong's slouch has lost her more attention than her lack of beauty. Even Sandy is critiscized for stooping. When you cross a room before people nine out of ten look at you and if you're straight and self contained and have a graceful atheletic carriage most of them will remark on it. In dancing it is very important to hold yourself well and remember to dance hard. Dancers like Betty and Grace and Alice *work hard*. Alice is an entirely self made dancer. At sixteen she was no better than you, but she practised and tried. A dancer like Elizabeth Clarkson looses partners. *You can not be lazy*. You should try not to trow a bit of weight on the man and keep your mind on it enough to follow well. If you'd spent the time on dancing with me as I've often asked you instead of playing the piano you'd be a good dancer. Louis Araway taught Kit to dance the Castle walk one summer and as long as it lasted she was almost rushed at dances. And dancing counts as nothing else does.

(3) Expression that is facial expression, is one of your weakest points. A girl of your good looks and at your age ought to have almost perfect control of her face. It ought to be almost like a mask

Written by me at 19 or so
Basis of Bernice

The General Subject of Conversation

Conversation like grace is a cultivated Art. Only to the very few does it come naturally. You are as you know, not a good conversationalist and you might very naturally ask, "What do boys like to talk about."

(1) Boys like to talk about themselves — much more than girls. A girl once named Helen Walcott, told me (and she was the most popular debutante in Washington the writer) that as soon as she got a man talking about himself she had him cinched and harnessed — they give themself away. Here are some leading questions for a girl to use.

a) You dance so much better than you did last year.

b) How about giving me that sporty necktie when you're thru with it.

c) You've got the longest eyelashes! (This will embarrass him, but he likes it)

d) I hear you've got a "line"!

e) Well who's your latest crush!

Avoid
a) When do you go back to school?

b) How long have you been home?

so that she'd have perfect control of any expression or impression she might wish to use.

(a) A good smile and one that could be assumed at will, is an absolute necesity. You smile on one side which is *absolutely wrong*. Get before a mirror and practise a smile and get a good one, a "radiant smile" ought to be in the facial vocubulary of every girl. Practise it—on girls, on the family. Practise doing it when you dont feel happy and when you're bored. When youre embarrassed, when you're at a disadvantage. Thats when you'll have to use it in society and when you've practised a thing in calm, then only are you sure of it as a good weapon in tight places

(b) A laugh isn't as important but its well to have a good one on ice. You natural one is very good, but your artificial one is bum. Next time you laugh naturally remember it and practise so you can do it any time you want. *Practise Anywhere.*

(c) A pathetic, appealing look is one every girl ought to have. Sandra and Ginevra are specialists at this: so is Ardita, Its best done by opening the eyes wide and drooping the mouth a little, looking upward (hanging the head a little) directly into the eyes of the man you're talking to. Ginevra and Sandra use this when getting of their "I'm so unpopular speeches and indeed they use it about half the time. Practise this.

(d) Dont bit or twist your lips—its sure death for any expression

(e) The two expressions *you have control over* now are *no good*. One is the side smile and the other is the thoughtful look with the eyes half closed.

I'm telling you this because Mother and I have absolutely no control over our facial expressions and we miss it. Mother's worse than I am—you know how people take advantage of what ever mood her face is in and kiḍ the life out of her. —Well you're young enough to get over it—tho' you're worse than I am now. The value of this practise is that whenever you're at a disadvantage you dont show it and boys hate to see a girl at a disadvantage.

Practise Now

Dress and Personality.

(A) No two people look alike in the same thing. but very few realize it. Shop keepers make money on the fact that the fat
Mrs. Jones will buy the hat that looked well on the thin Mrs.
Smith. You've got to find your type. To do so always look at
girls about your *size* and *coloring* and notice what they look
well in. Never buy so much as a sash without the most careful
consideration. *Study your type.* That is get your good points
and accentuate them. For instance you have very good fea-
tures—you ought to be able to wear jaunty hats and so forth.

(B) Almost all neatness is gained in man or woman by the arrangement of the hair. You have beautiful hair—you ought to be
able to do something with it. Go to the best groomed girl in
school and ask her and then wear it that way— Dont get
tired and changed unless you're sure the new way is better.
Catherine Tie is dowdy about her hair lately. Dont I notice
it? When Grace's hair looks well—she looks well When
its unkempt it looks like the devil. Sandy and Betty always
look neat and its their hair that does it.

(2)

(C) I'll line up your good points against your bad physically.

Good	Bad
Hair	Teeth only fair
Good General Size	Pale complexion
Good Features	Only fair figure
	Large hands and feet.

Now you see of the bad points only the last cannot be reme-
died. Now while slimness is a fashion you can cultivate it by
exercise— Find out how from some girl. Exercise would give
you a healthier skin. You should never rub cold cream into
your face because you have a slight tendency to grow hairs on
it. I'd find out about this from some Dr. who'd tell you what
you could use in place of a skin cream.

(D) A girl should always be careful about such things as under-skirt showing, long drawers showing under stockings, bad breath, mussy eyebrows (with such splendid eyebrows as yours you should brush them or wet them and train them every morning and night as I advised you to do long ago. They oughtn't to have a hair out of place.

(E) Walk and general physical grace. The point about this is that you'll be up against situations when ever you go out which will call for you to be graceful—not to physically clum-sey. Now you can only attain this by practise because it no more comes naturally to you than it does to me. Take some stylish walk you like and imitate it. A girl should have a little class. Look what a stylish walk Eleanor and Grace and Betty have and what a homely walk Marie and Alice have. Just because the first three deliberatly practised every where until now its so natural to them that they cant be ungraceful— This is true about every gesture. I noticed last Saturday that your gestures are awkward and so unnatural as to seem af-fected. Notice the way graceful girls hold their hands and feet. How they stoop, wave, run and then try because you cant practise those things when men are around. Its too late then. They ought to be secretive then

(F) General Summing Up.
(1) Dress scrupulously neatly and then forget your per-sonal appearance. Every stocking should be pulled up to the last wrinkle.
(2) Dont wear things like that fussy hat that aren't becom-ing to you— At least buy no more. Take someone who knows with you—some one who really knows.
(3) Conform to your type no matter what looks well in the store
(4) Cultivate deliberate physical grace. You'll never have it if you dont. I'll discuss dancing in a latter letter.

G. You see if you get any where and feel you look alright then there's one worry over and one bolt shot for self-confidence—and the person you're with, man, boy, woman, whether its Aunt Millie or Jack Allen or myself likes to feel that the person they're sponsoring is at least externally a credit. (The F. Scott Fitzgerald Papers)

Babes in the Woods

At the top of the stairs she paused. The emotions of divers on spring-boards, leading-ladies on opening nights, and lumpy, be-striped young men on the day of the Big Game, crowded through her. She felt as if she should have descended to a burst of drums or to a discordant blend of gems from Thaïs and Carmen. She had never been so worried about her appearance, she had never been so satisfied with it. She had been sixteen years old for two months.

"Isabelle!" called Elaine from her doorway.

"I'm ready," she caught a slight lump or nervousness in her throat.

"I've got on the wrong slippers and stockings—you'll have to wait a minute."

Isabelle started toward Elaine's door for a last peak at a mirror, but something decided her to stand there and gaze down the stairs. They curved tantalizingly and she could just catch a glimpse of two pairs of masculine feet in the hall below. Pump-shod in uniform black they gave no hint of identity, but eagerly she wondered if one pair were attached to Kenneth Powers. This young man, as yet unmet, had taken up a considerable part of her day—the first day of her arrival. Going up in the machine from the station Elaine had volunteered, amid a rain of questions and comment, revelation and exaggeration—

"Kenneth Powers is simply *mad* to meet you. He's stayed over a day from college and he's coming to-night. He's heard so much about you—"

It had pleased her to know this. It put them on more equal

terms, although she was accustomed to stage her own romances with or without a send-off. But following her delighted tremble of anticipation came a sinking sensation which made her ask:

"How do you mean he's heard about me? What sort of things?"

Elaine smiled—she felt more or less in the capacity of a showman with her more exotic guest.

"He knows you're good looking and all that." She paused— "I guess he knows you've been kissed."

Isabelle had shuddered a bit under the fur robe. She was accustomed to be followed by this, but it never failed to arouse in her the same feeling of resentment; yet—in a strange town it was an advantage. She was a speed, was she? Well? Let them find out. She wasn't quite old enough to be sorry nor nearly old enough to be glad.

"Anne (this was another schoolmate) told him, I didn't—I knew you wouldn't like it." Elaine had gone on naively. "She's coming over to-night to the dinner."

Out the window Isabelle watched the high-piled snow glide by in the frosty morning. It was ever so much colder here than in Pittsburg; the glass of the side door was iced and the windows were shirred with snow in the corners. Her mind played still with the one subject. Did he dress like that boy there who walked calmly down what was evidently a bustling business street, in moccasins and winter-carnival costume? How very *western!* Of course he wasn't that way: he went to college, was a freshman or something. Really she had no distinct idea of him. A two year back picture had not impressed her except by the big eyes, which he had probably grown up to by now. However in the last two weeks at school, when her Christmas visit to Elaine had been decided on, he had assumed the proportions of a worthy adversary. Children, the most astute of matchmakers, plot and plan quickly and Elaine had cleverly played a word sonata to Isabelle's excitable temperament. Isabelle was and had been for some time capable of very strong, if not very transient emotions.

They drew up at a spreading red stone building, set back from the snowy street. Mrs. Terrell greeted her rather impersonally and

Elaine's various younger brothers were produced from the corners where they skulked politely. Isabelle shook hands most tactfully. At her best she allied all with whom she came in contact. except older girls and some women. All the impressions that she made were conscious. The half dozen girls she met that morning were all rather impressed—and as much by her direct personality as by her reputation. Kenneth Powers seemed an unembarrased subject of conversation. Evidently he was a bit light of love. He was neither popular nor unpopular. Every girl there seemed to have had an affair with him at some time or other, but no one volunteered any really useful information. He was going to fall for her ... Elaine had issued that statement to her young set and they were retailing it back to Elaine as fast as they set eyes on Isabelle. Isabelle resolved mentally, that if necessary, she would force herself to like him—she owed it to Elaine. What if she were terribly disappointed. Elaine had painted him in such glowing colors—he was good looking, had a "line" and was properly inconstant. In fact he summed up all the romance that her age and environment led her to desire. Were those his dancing shoes that fox-trotted tentitavely around the soft rug below?

All impressions and in fact all ideas were terribly kaleidoscopic to Isabelle. She had that curious mixture of the social and artistic temperaments, found often in two classes, society women and actors. Her education, or rather her sophistication, had been absorbed from the boys who had dangled upon her favor, her tact was instinctive and her capacity for love affairs was limited only by the number of boys she met. Flirt smiled from her large, black-brown eyes and figured in her intense physical magnetism.

So she waited at the head of the stairs that evening while slippers and stockings were changed. Just as she was getting impatient Elaine came out beaming with her accustomed good nature and high spirits. Together they descended the broad stairs while the nervous searchlight of Isabelle's mind flashed on two ideas. She was glad she had high color to-night and she wondered if he danced well.

Downstairs the girls she had met in the afternoon surrounded her for a moment, looking unbelievably changed by the soft yellow light; then she heard Elaine's voice repeating a cycle of names and she found herself bowing to a sextette of black and white and terribly stiff figures. The name Powers figured somewhere, but she did not place him at first. A confused and very juvenile moment of awkward backings and bumpings, and everyone found themselves arranged talking to the very persons they least desired to. Isabelle manouvered herself and Peter Carroll, a sixth-former from Hotchkiss whom she had met that afternoon, to a seat at the piano. A reference, supposedly humorous, to the afternoon, was all she needed. What Isabelle could do socially with one idea was remarkable. First she repeated it rapturously in an enthusiastic contralto; then she held it off at a distance and smiled at it—her wonderful smile; then she delivered it in variations and played a sort of mental catch with it, all this in the nominal form of dialogue. Peter was fascinated and totally unconscious that this was being done not for him but for the black eyes that glistened under the shining, carefully watered hair a little to her left. As an actor even in the fullest flush of his own conscious magnetism gets a lasting impression of most of the people in the front row, so Isabelle sized up Kenneth Powers. First, he was of middle height, and from her feeling of disappointment, she knew that she had expected him to be tall and of Vernon Castle-ish slenderness. His hair and eyes were his most noticeable possessions—they were black and they fairly glittered. For the rest, he had rather dark skin with a faint flush, and a straight romantic profile, the effect set off by a close-fitting dress suit and a silk ruffled shirt of the kind that women still delight in on men, but men were just beginning to get tired of.

Kenneth was just quietly smiling.

"Don't *you* think so?" she said suddenly, turning to him innocent eyed.

There was a stir near the door and Elaine led the way to dinner. Kenneth struggled to her side and whispered:

"You're my dinner partner—Isabelle."

Isabelle gasped—this was rather quick work. Of course it made it more interesting, but really she felt as if a good line had been taken from the star and given to a minor character. She mustn't lose the leadership a bit. The dinner table glittered with laughter at the confusion of getting places and then curious eyes were turned on her, sitting near the head. She was enjoying this immensely, and Peter Carroll was so engrossed with the added sparkle of her rising color that he forgot to pull out Elaine's chair and fell into a dim confusion. Kenneth was on the other side, full of confidence and vanity, looking at her most consciously. He started directly and so did Peter.

"I've heard a lot about you—"

"Wasn't it funny this afternoon—"

Both stopped. Isabelle turned to Kenneth shyly. Her face was always enough answer for anyone, but she decided to speak.

"How—who from?"

"From everybody—for years." She blushed appropriately. On her right Peter was hors-de-combat already, although he hadn't quite realized it.

"I'll tell you what I thought about you when I first saw you," Kenneth continued. She leaned slightly toward him and looked modestly at the celery before her. Peter sighed—he knew Kenneth and the situations that Kenneth was born to handle. He turned to Elaine and asked her when she was going back to school.

II.

Isabelle and Kenneth were distinctly not innocent, nor were they particularly hardened. Morover, amateur standing had very little value in the game they were beginning to play. They were simply very sophisticated, very calculating and finished, young actors, each playing a part that they had played for years. They had both started with good looks and excitable temperaments and the rest was the result of certain accesable popular novels, and dressing-room conversation culled from a slightly older set. When Isabelle's eyes, wide and innocent, proclaimed the ingenue most, Kenneth was proportionally less deceived. He waited for the mask to drop off, but at the same time he did not question her right to wear it. She, on her part, was not impressed by his studied air of blase sophistication. She came from a larger city and had slightly an advantage in range. But she accepted his pose. It was one of the dozen little conventions of this kind of affair. He was aware that he was getting this particular favor now because she had been coached. He knew that he stood for merely the best thing in sight, and that he would have to improve his opportunity before he lost his advantage. So they proceeded, with an infinite guile that would have horrified the parents of both.

After dinner the party swelled to forty and there was dancing in a large ex-play-room downstairs. Everything went smoothly—boys cut in on Isabelle every few feet and then squabbled in the corners with: "You might let me get more than an *inch*," and "She didn't like it either—she told me so next time I cut in." It was true—she told everyone so, and gave every hand a parting pressure that said "You know that your dances are *making* my evening."

But time passed, two hours of it and the less subtle beaux had better learned to focus their pseudo-passionate glances elsewhere for eleven o'clock found Isabelle and Kenneth on a leather lounge in a little den off the music-room. She was conscious that they were a handsome pair and seemed to belong distinctivly on this leather lounge while lesser lights fluttered and chattered down stairs. Boys who passed the door looked in enviously—girls who passed only laughed and frowned, and grew wise within themselves.

They had now reached a very definite stage. They had traded ages, eighteen and sixteen. She had listened to much that she had heard before. He was a freshman at college, sang in the glee club and expected to make the freshman hockey-team. He had learned that some of the boys she went with in Pittsburg were "terrible speeds" and came to parties intoxicated—most of them were nineteen or so, and drove alluring Stutzes. A good half of them seemed to have already flunked out of various boarding schools and colleges, but some of them bore good collegiate names that made him feel rather young. As a matter of fact Isabelle's acquaintance with college boys was mostly through older cousins. She had bowing acquaintance with a lot of young men who thought she was "a pretty kid" and "worth keeping an eye on." But Isabelle strung the names into a fabrication of gaiety that would have dazzled a Viennese nobleman. Such is the power of young contralto voices on leather sofas.

I have said that they had reached a very definite stage—nay more—a very critical stage. Kenneth had stayed over a day to meet her and his train left at twelve-eighteen that night. His trunk and suitcase awaited him at the station and his watch was already beginning to worry him and hang heavy in his pocket.

"Isabelle," he said suddenly. I want to tell you something." They had been talking lightly about "that funny look in her eyes," and on the relative merits of dancing and sitting out, and Isabelle knew from the change in his manner exactly what was coming—indeed she had been wondering how soon it would come. Kenneth reached above their heads and turned out the electric light so that they were in the dark except for the glow from the red lamps that fell through the door from the music room. Then he began:

"I don't know—I don't know whether or not you know what you—what I'm going to say. Lordy Isabelle—this sounds like a line but it isn't."

"I know," said Isabelle softly.

"I may never see you again—I have darned hard luck sometimes." He was leaning away from her on the other arm of the lounge, but she could see his black eyes plainly in the dark.

"You'll see me again—silly." There was just the slightest emphasis on the last word—so that it became almost a term of endearment. He continued a bit huskily:

"I've fallen for a lot of people—girls—and I guess you have too—boys, I mean but honestly you—" he broke off suddenly and leaned forward, chin on his hands, a favorite and studied gesture. "Oh what's the use, you'll go your way and I suppose I'll go mine."

Silence for a moment. Isabelle was quite stirred—she wound her handkerchief into a tight ball and by the faint light that streamed over her, dropped it deliberately on the floor. Their hands touched for an instant but neither spoke. Silences were becoming more frequent and more delicious. Outside another stray couple had come up and were experimenting on the piano. After the usual preliminary of "chopsticks," one of them started "Babes in the Woods" and a light tenor carried the words into the den—

> "Give me your hand
> I'll understand
> We're off to slumberland."

Isabelle hummed it softly and trembled as she felt Kenneth's hand close over hers.

"Isabelle," he whispered. "You know I'm mad about you. You *do* give a darn about me."

"Yes."

"How much do you care—do you like anyone better?"

"No." He could scarcely hear her, although he bent so near that he felt her breath against his cheek.

"Isabelle, we're going back to school for six long months and why shouldn't we—if I could only just have one thing to remember you by—."

"Close the door." Her voice had just stirred so that he half wondered whether she had spoken at all. As he swung the door softly shut, the music seemed quivering just outside.

> "Moonlight is bright
> Kiss me good-night."

What a wonderful song she thought—everything was wonderful to-night, most of all this romantic scene in the den with their hands clinging and the inevitable looming charmingly close. The future vista of her life seemed an unended succession of scenes like this, under moonlight and pale starlight, and in the backs of warm limousines and in low cosy roadsters stopped under sheltering trees—only the boy might change, and this one was so nice.

"Isabelle!" His whisper blended in the music and they seemed to float nearer together. Her breath came faster. "Can't I kiss you Isabelle—Isabelle?" Lips half parted, she turned her head to him in the dark. Suddenly the ring of voices, the sound of running footsteps surged toward them. Like a flash Kenneth reached up and turned on the light and when the door opened and three boys, the wrathy and dance-craving Peter among them, rushed in, he was turning over the magazines on the table, while she sat, without moving, serene and unembarrassed, and even greeted them with a welcoming smile. But her heart was beating wildly and she felt somehow as if she had been deprived.

It was evidently over. There was a clamour for a dance, there was a glance that passed between them, on his side, despair, on hers, regret, and then the evening went on, with the reassured beaux and the eternal cutting in.

At quarter to twelve Kenneth shook hands with her gravely, in a crowd assembled to wish him good-speed. For an instant he lost his poise and she felt slightly foolish, when a satirical voice from a concealed wit on the edge of the company cried:

"Take her outside, Kenneth." As he took her hand he pressed it a little and she returned the pressure as she had done to twenty hands that evening—that was all.

At two o'clock upstairs Elaine asked her if she and Kenneth had had a "time" in the den. Isabelle turned to her quietly. In her eyes was the light of the idealist, the inviolate dreamer of Joan-like dreams.

"No!" she answered. "I don't do that sort of thing any more—he asked me to, but I said 'No.'"

As she crept into bed she wondered what he'd say in his special delivery to-morrow. He had such a good looking mouth—would she ever—?

"Fourteen angels were watching over them" sang Elaine sleepily from the next room.

"Damn!" muttered Isabelle and punched the pillow into a lucurious lump—"Damn!"

Sentiment—and the Use of Rouge

"Sentiment—and the Use of Rouge" treats pressing topical issues. For instance, the following sentence would be borrowed from it to summarize the pessimistic confusion of *This Side of Paradise*: "Damned muddle—everything a muddle, everybody off-side, and the referee gotten rid of—everybody trying to say that if the referee were there he'd have been on their side." And "the problem of sex," which appears here neither as the criminal act of "Tarquin of Cheepside" nor the adolescent game of "Babes in the Woods," causes the hero of the novel to experience terrifying hallucinations and becomes synonymous with "the problem of evil."

Like many of his contemporaries, Scott Fitzgerald came to believe that the generation of the nineties through its philosophy of "personal selfishness and national conceit" had led its progeny into the great war. The protagonist of *This Side of Paradise* writes: "Victorians, Victorians, who never learned to weep/who sowed the bitter harvest that your children go to reap." (p. 164) Whereas the young entered the war feeling they would make the world safe for democracy, they soon learned that they were "dying in the Argonne for a phrase that was empty before their bodies withered." ("The Smilers," *Saturday Evening Post*, October 19, 1929) A soldier on his way to camp is described in *The Beautiful and Damned*: "It was wearisome to contemplate that animate protoplasm, reasonable by courtesy only, shut up in a car by an incomprehensible civilization, taken somewhere, to do a vague something without aim or significance or consequence." (p. 315)

One important traditional value that was rejected but never re-

141

placed by the young was religious faith. And, as with religion, so with politics. Increased awareness of the ineptitude and corruption of the political system on the part of the young, although good in itself, did not lead to happiness.

Of the new sexual values, Scott Fitzgerald disapproved on two counts. Romanticist as he was, he based relations between men and women primarily on spiritual qualities. As a moralist, he felt that monogamy represented "the simplest solution of the mating instinct" and "the most completely satisfactory state of being in this somewhat depressing world." (*New York American*, February 24, 1924) An article called "Girls Believe in Girls" analyzes the changes in sexual standards. First, there had been the birth of the flapper: "Back in 1912 the Castles, by making modern dancing respectable, brought the nice girl into the cabaret and set her down next to the distinctly not-nice girl. At that moment the Era of the Flapper was born." Later, during the war, "some ten commandments crashed . . . and afterwards there was a demand not to be let down from its excitement." By 1922 the "flapper movement," which, actually, was little more than the facing of some "questionable biological data," was over. As a result of all this, "the identification of virtue with chastity no longer exists among girls over twenty." (*Liberty*, February 8, 1930)

Although Fitzgerald favored an honest recognition of the sexual facts of life and the newly won freedom of women, he objected to the loosening of morals attendant upon the new honesty and the new freedom—as is evidenced in "Sentiment—and the Use of Rouge." America might be headed for "the greatest, gaudiest spree in history," but he could not share its naïve optimism. All the plots he thought of "had a touch of disaster in them." He anticipated that lovely girls would go to ruin, that wealth would disintegrate, that millionaires would be "beautiful and damned." ("Early Success," *American Cavalcade*, October, 1937)

Scott Fitzgerald considered himself a moralist, as certainly he was. He tells us he had "a New England conscience—developed in Minnesota" ("One Hundred False Starts," *Saturday Evening*

Post, March 4, 1933) and, in spite of his opposition to school-teachers, there was just the ghost of one in him. He explains in a letter of 1939: "I guess I am too much a moralist at heart and really want to preach at people in some acceptable form rather than to entertain them." (*The Letters of F. Scott Fitzgerald*, p. 63)

These revelations are consistent with the point of view expressed as early as February, 1917. In "The Spire and the Gargoyle," Fitzgerald had stated that while epicureanism had been "romantic" during his Princeton days, it was "rather disgusting in the city" because "it was much too easy; it lacked the penance of the five o'clock morning train back to college."

Sentiment—and the Use of Rouge

I.

This story has no moral value. It is about a man who had fought for two years and how he came back to England for two days, and then how he went away again. It is unfortunately one of those stories which must start at the beginning, and the beginning consists merely of a few details. There were two brothers (two sons of Lord Blachford) who sailed to Europe with the first hundred thousand. Lieutenant Richard Harrington Syneforth, the elder, was killed in some forgotten raid; the younger, Lieutenant Clay Harrington Syneforth is the hero of this story. He was now a Captain in the Seventeenth Sussex and the immoral thing in the story happens to him. The important part to remember is that when his father met him at Paddington station and drove him up town in his motor, he hadn't been in England for two years—and this was in the early spring of nineteen-seventeen. Various circumstances had brought this about, wounds, advancement, meeting his family in Paris, and mostly being twenty-two and anxious to show his company an example of indefatigable energy. Besides, most of his friends were dead and he had rather a horror of seeing the gaps they'd leave in his England. And here is the story.

He sat at dinner and thought himself rather stupid and unnecessarily moody as his sister's light chatter amused the table, Lord and Lady Blachford, himself and two unsullied aunts. In the first place he was rather doubtful about his sister's new manner. She seemed, well, perhaps a bit loud and theatrical, and she was certainly pretty enough not to need so much paint. She couldn't be more than eighteen, and paint—it seemed so useless. Of course he was used to it in his mother, would have been shocked had she appeared in her unrouged furrowedness, but on Clara it merely accentuated her youth. Altogether he had never seen such obvious paint, and, as they had always been a shockingly frank family, he told her so.

"You've got too much stuff on your face." He tried to speak casually and his sister nothing wroth, jumped up and ran to a mirror.

"No, I haven't," she said, calmly returning.

"I thought," he continued rather annoyed, "that the criterion of how much paint to put on, was whether men were sure you'd used any or not."

His sister and mother exchanged glances and both spoke at once.

"Not now, Clay, you know——" began Clara.

"Really, Clay," interrupted his mother, "you don't know exactly what the standards are, so you can't quite criticize. It happens to be a fad to paint a little more."

Clayton was now rather angry.

"Will all the women at Mrs. Severance's dance tonight be striped like this?"

Clara's eyes flashed.

"Yes!"

"Then I don't believe I care to go."

Clara, about to flare up, caught her mother's eye and was silent.

"Clay, I want you to go," said Lady Blachford hastily. "People want to see you before they forget what you look like. And for tonight let's not talk about war or paint."

In the end Clay went. A navy subaltran called for his sister at ten and he followed in lonesome state at half-past. After half an hour he had had all he wanted. Frankly, the dance seemed all wrong. He remembered Mrs. Severance's ante-bellum affairs—staid, correct occasions they were, with only a mere scattering from the faster set, just those people who couldn't possibly be left out. Now it all was blent, some how, in one set. His sister had not exaggerated, practically every girl there was painted, overpainted; girls whom he remembered as curate-hunters, holders of long conversations with earnest young men on incence and the validity of orders, girls who had been terrifyingly masculine and had talked about dances as if they were the amusement of the feeble-minded—all were there, trotting through the most extreme steps from over the water. He danced stiffly with many who had delighted his youth, and he found that he wasn't enjoying himself at all. He found that he had come to picture England as a land of sorrow and acetisism and while there was little extravagance displayed tonight, he thought that the atmosphere had fallen to that of artificial gayety rather than risen to a stern calmness. Even under the carved, gilt ceiling of the Severances' there was strangely an impression of dance-hall rather than dance, people arrived and departed most informally and, oddly enough, there was a dearth of older people rather than of younger. But there was something in the very faces of the girls, something which was half enthusiasm and half recklessness, that depressed him more than any concrete thing.

When he had decided this and had about made up his mind to go, Eleanor Marbrooke came in. He looked at her keenly. She had not lost, not a bit. He fancied that she had not quiet so much paint on as the others, and when he and she talked he felt a social refuge in her cool beauty. Even then he felt that the difference between she and the others was in degree rather than in kind. He stayed, of course, and one o'clock found them sitting apart, watching. There had been a drifting away and now there seemed to be nothing but officers and girls; the Severances themselves seemed out of place as they chattered volubly in a corner to a young couple who looked as if they would rather be left alone.

"Eleanor," he demanded, "why is it that everyone looks so— well, so loose—so socially slovenly?"

"It's terribly obvious, isn't it?" she agreed, following his eyes around the room.

"And no one seems to care" he continued.

"No one does," she responded, "but my dear man, we can't sit here and criticize our hosts. What about me? How do I look?"

He regarded her critically.

"I'd say on the whole, that you've kept your looks."

"Well, I like that," she raised her brows at him in reproof. "You talk as if I were some shelved, old play-about, just over some domestic catastrophy."

There was a pause; then he asked her directly.

"How about Dick?"

She grew serious at once.

"Poor Dick—I suppose we were engaged."

"Suppose," he said astonished, "why it was understood by everyone, both our families knew. I know I used to lie awake and envy my lucky brother."

She laughed.

"Well, we certainly thought ourselves engaged. If war hadn't come we'd be comfortably married now, but if he were still alive under these circumstances, I doubt if we'd be even engaged."

"You weren't in love with him?"

"Well, you see, perhaps that wouldn't be the question, perhaps he wouldn't marry me and perhaps I *wouldn't* marry him."

He jumped to his feet astounded and her warning hush just prevented him from exclaiming aloud. Before he could control his voice enough to speak she had whisked off with a staff officer. What could she mean?—except that in some moment of emotional excitement she had—but he couldn't bear to think of Eleanor in that light. He must have misunderstood—he must talk more with her. No, surely—if it had been true she wouldn't have said it so casually. He watched her—how close she danced. Her bright brown hair lay against the staff officer's shoulder and her vivacious face was only two or three inches from his when she talked. All things considered Clay was becoming more angry every minute with things in general.

Next time he danced with her she seized his arm, and before he knew her intention, they had said goodbyes to the Severances' and were speeding away in Eleanor's limousine.

"It's a nineteen-thirteen car—imagine having a four year old limousine before the war."

"Terrific privation," he said ironically. "Eleanor, I want to speak to you—"

"And I to you. That's why I took you away. Where are you living?"

"At home."

"Well then we'll go to your old rooms in Grove Street. You've still got them, haven't you?"

Before he could answer she had spoken to the chauffer and was leaning back in the corner smiling at him.

"Why Eleanor, we can't do that—talk there—."

"Are the rooms cleaned?" she interrupted.

"About once a month I think, but—."

"That's all that's necessary. In fact it'll be wonderfully proper, won't be clothes lying around the room as there usually are at bachelor teas. At Colonel Hotesane's farewell party, Gertrude Evarts and I saw—in the middle of the floor, well, my dear, a series of garments and—as we were the first to arrive we—."

"Eleanor," said Clay firmly, "I don't like this."

"I know you don't, and that's why we're going to your rooms to talk it over. Good heavens, do you think people worry these days about where conversations take place, unless they're in wireless towers, or shoreways in coast towns?"

The machine had stopped and before he could bring further argument to bear she had stepped out and scurried up the steps, where she announced that she would wait until he came and opened the door. He had no alternative. He followed, and as they mounted the stairs inside he could hear her laughing softly at him in the darkness.

He threw open the door and groped for the electric light, and in the glow that followed both stood without moving. There on the table sat a picture of Dick, Dick almost as they had last seen him, worldly wise and sophisticated, in his civilian clothes. Eleanor was the first to move. She crossed swiftly over, the dust rising with the swish of her silk, and elbows on the table said softly:

"Poor old handsome, with your beautiful self all smashed." She turned to Clay "Dick didn't have much of a soul, such a small soul. He never bothered about eternity and I doubt if he knows any—but he had a way with him, and oh, that magnificent body of his, red gold hair, brown eyes—" her voice trailed off and she sank lazily onto the sofa in front of the hearth.

"Build a fire and then come and put your arm around me and we'll talk." Obediently he searched for wood while she sat and chatted. "I won't pretend to busybody around and try to help— I'm far too tired. I'm sure I can give the impression of home much better by just sitting here and talking, can't I?"

He looked up from where he knelt at her feet manipulating the kerosene can, and realized that his voice was husky as he spoke.

"Just talk about England—about the country a little and about Scotland and tell me things that have happened, amusing provincial things and things with women in them—put yourself in" he finished rather abruptly.

Eleanor smiled and kneeling down beside him lit the match and ran it along the edge of the paper that undermined the logs. She twisted her head to read it as it curled up in black at the corners, "August 14th, 1915. Zeppelin raid in—there it goes" as it disappeared in little, licking flames. "My little sister—you remember Katherine; Kitty, the one with the yellow hair and the little lisp—she was killed by one of those things—she and a governess, that summer."

"Little Kitty," he said sadly, "a lot of children were killed I know, a lot, I didn't know she was gone," he was far away now and a set look had come into his eyes. She hastened to change the subject.

"Lots—but we're not on death tonight. We're going to pretend we're happy. Do you see?" She patted his knee reprovingly, "we *are* happy. We *are!* Why you were almost whimsical awhile ago. I believe you're a sentimentalist. Are you?

He was still gazing absently at the fire but he looked up at this.

"Tonight, I am—almost—for the first time in my life. Are you, Eleanor?"

"No, I'm romantic. There's a huge difference; a sentimental person thinks things will last, a romantic person hopes they wont."

He was in a reverie again and she knew that he had hardly heard her.

"Excuse please," she pleaded, slipping close to him. "Do be a nice boy and put your arm around me." He put his arm gingerly about until she began to laugh quietly. When he hastily withdrew it, and bending forward, talked quickly at the fire.

"Will you tell me why in the name of this mad world we're here tonight? Do you realize that this is—was a bachelor apartment before the bachelors all married the red widow over the channel—and you'll be compromised?"

She seized the straps of his shoulder belt and tugged at him until his grey eyes looked into hers.

"Clay, Clay, don't—you musn't use small petty words like that at this time. Compromise! What's that to words like Life and Love and Death and England. Compromise! Clay I don't believe anyone uses that word except servants." She laughed. "Clay, you and our butler are the only men in England who use the word compromise. My maid and I have been warned within a week— How odd—Clay, look at me."

He looked at her and saw what she intended, beauty heightened by enthusiasm. Her lips were half parted in a smile, her hair just so slightly disarranged.

"Damned witch," he muttered. "You used to read Tolstoy, and believe him."

"Did I?" her gaze wandered to the fire. "So I did, so I did." Then her eyes came back to him and the present. "Really, Clay, we must stop gazing at the fire. It puts our minds on the past and tonight there's got to be no past or future, no time, just tonight, you and I sitting here and I most tired for a military shoulder to rest my head upon." But he was off on an old tack thinking of Dick and he spoke his thoughts aloud.

"You used to talk Tolstoy to Dick and I thought it was scandalous for such a good-looking girl to be intellectual."

"I wasn't, really," she admitted. "It was to impress Dick."

"I was shocked, too, when I read something of Tolstoy's, I struck the something Sonata."

"Kreutzer Sonata," she suggested.

"That's it. I thought it was immoral for young girls to read Tolstoy and told Dick so. He used to nag me about that. I was nineteen."

"Yes, we thought you quite the young prig. We considered ourselves advanced."

"You're only twenty, aren't you?" asked Clay suddenly. She nodded.

"Don't you believe in Tolstoy any more?" he asked, almost fiercely.

She shook her head and then looked up at him almost wistfully.

"Won't you let me lean against your shoulder just the smallest bit?" He put his arm around her, never once taking his eyes from her face, and suddenly the whole strength of her appeal burst upon him. Clay was no saint, but he had always been rather decent about women. Perhaps that's why he felt so helpless now. His emotions were not complex. He knew what was wrong, but he knew also that he wanted this woman, this warm creature of silk and life who crept so close to him. There were reasons why he oughtn't to have her, but he had suddenly seen how love was a big word like Life and Death, and she knew that he realized and was glad. Still they sat without moving for a long while and watched the fire.

II.

At two-twenty next day Clay shook hands gravely with his father and stepped into the train for Dover. Eleanor, comfortable with a novel, was nestled into a corner of his compartment, and as he entered she smiled a welcome and closed the book.

"Well," she began. I felt like a minion of the almighty secret service as I slid by your inspiring and impecable father, swathed in yards and yards of veiling."

"He wouldn't have noticed you without your veil," answered Clayton, sitting down. "He was really most emotional under

all that brusqueness. Really, you know he's quite a nice chap. Wish
I knew him better."

The train was in motion; the last uniforms had drifted in like
brown, blown leaves, and now it seemed as if one tremendous
wind was carrying them shoreward.

"How far are you going with me?" asked Clayton.

"Just to Rochester, an hour and a half. I absolutely had to
see you before you left, which isn't very Spartan of me. But
really, you see, I feel that you don't quite understand about last
night, and look at me, as" she paused "well—as rather exceptional."

"Wouldn't I be rather an awful cad if I thought about it in
those terms at all?"

"No," she said cheerily, "I, for instance, am both a romantiscist
and a psychologist. It does take the romance out of anything to
analyze it, but I'm going to do it if only to clear myself in your
eyes."

"You don't have to—" he began.

"I know I don't," she interrupted, "but I'm going to, and when
I've finished you'll see where weakness and inevitability shade off.
No, I don't believe in Zola."

"I don't know him."

"Well, my dear, Zola said that environment is environment,
but he referred to families and races, and this is the story of a
class."

"What class?"

"Our class."

"Please," he said, "I've been wanting to hear.

She settled herself against his shoulder, and gazing out at the
vanishing country, began to talk very deliberately.

"It was said, before the war, that England was the only country
in the world where women weren't safe from men of their own
class."

"One particular fast set," he broke in.

"A set, my dear man, who were fast but who kept every bit of
their standing and position. You see even that was reaction. The
idea of physical fitness came in with the end of the Victorians.

Drinking died down in the Universities. Why you yourself once told me that the really bad men never drank, rather kept themselves fit for moral or intellectual crimes."

"It was rather Victorian to drink much," he agreed. "Chaps who drank were usually young fellows about to become curates, sowing the conventional wild oats by the most orthodox tippling."

"Well," she continued, "there had to be an outlet—and there was, and you know the form it took in what you called the fast set. Next enter Mr. Mars. You see as long as there was moral pressure exerted, the rotten side of society was localized. I won't say it wasn't spreading, but it was spreading slowly, some people even thought, rather normally, but when men began to go away and not come back, when marriage became a hurried thing and widows filled London, and all traditions seemed broken, why then things were different."

"How did it start?"

"It started in cases where men were called away hurriedly and girls lost their nerve. Then the men didn't come back—and there were the girls.—."

He gasped.

"That was going on at the beginning?—I didn't know at all."

"Oh it was very quiet at first. Very little leaked out into daylight, but the thing spread in the dark. The next thing, you see was to weave a sentimental mantle to throw over it. It was there and it had to be excused. Most girls either put on trousers and drove cars all day or painted their faces and danced with officers all night."

"And what mighty principle had the honor of being a cloak for all that?" he asked sarcastically.

"Now here, you see, is the paradox. I can talk like this and pretend to analyze, and even sneer at the principle. Yet I'm as much under the spell as the most wishy-washy typist who spends a week end at Brighton with her young man before he sails with the conscripts."

"I'm waiting to hear what the spell is."

"It's this—self sacrifice with a capitol S. Young men going to get killed for us.—We would have been their wives—we can't be —therefore we'll be as much as we can. And that's the story."

"Good God!"

"Young officer comes back," she went on; "must amuse him, must amuse him; must give him the impression that people here are with him, that it's a big home he's coming to, that he's appreciated. Now you know, of course, in the lower classes that sort of thing means children. Whether that will ever spread to us will depend on the duration of the war."

"How about old ideas, and standards of woman and that sort of thing?" he asked, rather sheepishly.

"Sky-high, my dear—dead and gone. It might be said for utility that it's better and safer for the race that officers stay with women of their own class. Think of the next generation in France."

To Clay the whole compartment had suddenly become smothering. Bubbles of conventional ethics seemed to have burst and the long stagnant gas was reaching him. He was forced to seize his mind and make it cling to whatever shreds of the old still floated on the moral air. Eleanor's voice came to him like the grey creed of a new materialistic world, the contrast was the more vivid because of the remains of errotic honor and sentimental religiosity that she flung out with the rest.

"So you see, my dear, utility, heroism and sentiment all combine and *levoice*. And we're pulling into Rochester," she turned to him pathetically. "I see that in trying to clear myself I've only indicted my whole sex," and with tears in their eyes they kissed.

On the platform they talked for half a minute more. There was no emotion. She was trying to analyze again and her smooth brow was wrinkled in the effort. He was endeavoring to digest what she had said, but his brain was in a whirl.

"Do you remember," he asked, "what you said last night about love being a big word like Life and Death?"

"A regular phrase; part of the technique of—of the game; a catch word." The train moved off and as Clay swung himself on the last car she raised her voice so that he could hear her to the last—"*Love* is a big word, but I was flattering us. Real Love's as big as Life and Death, but not that love—not that—" Her voice failed and mingled with the sound of the rails, and to Clay she seemed to fade out like a grey ghost on the platform.

III.

When the charge broke and the remnants lapped back like spent waves, Sergeant O'Flaherty, a bullet through the left side, dropped beside him, and as weary castaways fight half listlessly for shore, they crawled and pushed and edged themselves into a shell crater. Clay's shoulder and back were bleeding profusely and he searched heavily and clumsily for his first aid package.

"That'll be that the Seventeenth Sussex gets reorganized," remarked O'Flaherty, sagely. "Two weeks in the rear and two weeks home."

"Damn good regiment, it was, O'Flaherty," said Clay. They would have seemed like two philosophic majors commenting from safe behind the lines had it not been that Clay was flat on his back, his face in a drawn ecstasy of pain, and that the Irishman was most evidently bleeding to death. The latter was twining an improvised tourniquet on his thigh, watching it with the careless casual interest a bashful suitor bestows upon his hat.

"I can't get up no emotion over a regiment these nights," he commented disgustedly. "This'll be the fifth I was in that I seen smashed to hell. I joined these Sussex byes so I needn't see more o' me own go."

"I think you know every one in Ireland, Sergeant.

"All Ireland's me friend, Captain, though I niver knew it 'till I left. So I left the Irish, what was left of them. You see when an English bye dies he does some play actin' before. Blood ,on an Englishman always calls rouge to me mind. It's a game with him. The Irish take death damn serious."

Clayton rolled painfully over and watched the night come softly down and blend with the drifting smoke. They were certainly between the devil and the deep sea and the slang of the next generation will use "no man's land" for that. O'Flaherty was still talking.

"You see you has to do somethin'. You haven't any God worth remarkin' on. So you pass from life in the names of your holy principles, and hope to meet in Westminster."

"We're not mystics, O'Flaherty," muttered Clay, "but we've got a firm grip on God and reality."

"Mystics, my eye, beggin' your pardon, lieutenant," cried the Irishman, "a mystic ain't no race, it's a saint. You got the most airy way o' thinkin' in the wurruld an yit you talk about plain faith as if it was cloud gazin'. There was a lecture last week behind Vimy Y. M. C. A., an' I stuck my head in the door; 'Tan-gi-ble,' the fellow was sayin' 'we must be Tan-gi-ble in our religion, we must be practicle' an' he starts off on Christian brotherhood an' honorable death—so I stuck me head out again. An' you got lots a good men dyin' for that every day—tryin' to be tangi-ble, dyin' because their father's a Duke or because he ain't. But that ain't what I got to think of. An' right here let's light a pipe before it gets dark enough for the damn burgomasters to see the match and practice on it."

Pipes, as indispensible as the hard ration, were going in no time, and the sergeant continued as he blew a huge lung full of smoke towards the earth with incongruous supercaution.

"I fight because I like it, an' God ain't to blame for that, but when it's death you're talkin' about I'll tell you what I get an' you don't. Pere Dupont gets in front of the Frenchies an' he says: 'Allon, mes enfants!' fine! an' Father O'Brien, he says: 'Go on in byes and bate the Luther out o' them'—great stuff! But can you see the reverent Updike—Updike just out o' Oxford, yellin' 'mix it up, chappies,' or 'soak 'em blokes?'—No, Captain, the best leader you ever get is a six foot rowin' man that thinks God's got a seat in the House o' Commons. All sportin' men have to have a bunch o' cheerin' when they die. Give an Englishman four inches in the sportin' page this side of the whistle an' he'll die happy—but not O'Flaherty."

But Clay's thoughts were far away. Half delirious, his mind wandered to Eleanor. He had thought of nothing else for a week, ever since their parting at Rochester, and so many new sides of what he had learned were opening up. He had suddenly realized about Dick and Eleanor, they must have been married to all intents and purposes. Of course Clay had written to Eleanor from Paris, asking her to marry him on his return, and just yesterday he had gotten a very short, very kind, but definite refusal. And he couldn't understand at all.

Then there was his sister—Eleanor's words still rang in his ear. "They either put on trousers and act as chauffers all day or put on paint and dance with officers all night." He felt perfectly sure that Clara was still well—virtuous. Virtuous—what a ridiculous word it seemed, and how odd to be using it about his sister. Clara had always been so painfully good. At fourteen she had been sent to Boston for a souvenir picture of Louisa M. Alcott to hang over her bed. His favorite amusement had been to replace it by some startling soubrette in tights, culled from the pages of the *Pink Un*. Well Clara, Eleanor, Dick, he himself, were all in the same boat, no matter what the actuality of their innocence or guilt. If he ever got back—.

The Irishman, evidently sinking fast, was talking rapidly.

"Put your wishy-washy pretty clothes on everythin' but it ain't no disguise. If I get drunk it's the flesh and the devil, if you get drunk it's your wild oats. But you ain't disguisin' death, not to me you ain't. It's a damn serious affair. I may get killed for me flag, but I'm goin' to die for meself. 'I die for England' he says. 'Settle up with God, you're through with England' I says."

He raised himself on his elbow and shook his fist toward the German trenches.

"It's you an' your damn Luther," he shouted. "You been protestin' and analyzin' until you're makin' my body ache and burn like hell; you been evolvin' like mister Darwin, an' you stretched yourself so far that you've split. Everythin's in-tan-gi-ble except your God. Honor an' Fatherland an' Westminster Abbey, they're all in-tan-gi-ble except God an' sure you got him tan-gi-ble. You got him on the flag an' in the constitution. Next you'll be writin' your bibles with Christ sowin' wild oats to make him human. You say he's on your side. Onc't, just onc't, he had a favorite nation and they hung Him up by the hands and feet and his body hurt him and burn't him," his voice grew fainter. "Hail Mary, full of grace, the Lord is wit' thee—." His voice trailed off, he shuddered and was dead.

The hours went on. Clayton lit another pipe, heedless of what German sharpshooters might see. A heavy March mist had come down and the damp was eating into him. His whole left side was paralyzed and he felt chill creep slowly over him. He spoke aloud.

"Damned old mist—damned lucky old Irishman—Damnation." He felt a dim wonder that he was to know death but his thoughts turned as ever to England, and three faces came in sequence before him. Clara's, Dick's and Eleanor's. It was all such a mess. He'd like to have gone back and finished that conversation. It had stopped at Rochester—he had stopped living in the station at Rochester. How queer to have stopped there—Rochester had no significance. Wasn't there a play where a man was born in a station, or a handbag in a station, and he'd stopped living at— what did the Irishman say about cloaks, Eleanor said something about cloaks; too, he couldn't see any cloaks, didn't feel sentimental—only cold and dim and mixed up. He didn't know about God—God was a good thing for curates—then there was the Y. M. C. A. God—and he always wore short sleeves, and bumpy Oxfords—but that wasn't God—that was just the man who talked about God to soldiers. And then there was O'Flaherty's God. He felt as if he knew him, but then he'd never called him God— he was fear and love, and it wasn't dignified to fear God—or even to love him except in a calm respectable way. There were so many God's it seemed—he had thought that Christianity was monotheistic, and it seemed pagan to have so many Gods.

Well, he'd find out the whole muddled business in about three minutes, and a lot of good it'd do anybody else left in the muddle.

Damned muddle—everything a muddle, everybody offside, and the referee gotten rid of—everybody trying to say that if the referee were there he'd have been on their side. He was going to go and find that old referee—find him—get hold of him, get a good hold—cling to him—cling to him—ask him—.

The Pierian Springs
and the Last Straw

Scott Fitzgerald's experimentation with narrative focus in the apprentice fiction is a good example of the author as an incipient artist, for most serious literary craftsmen—consciously or unconsciously—attempt to present events from the most effective point of view.

Five of the prep-school pieces employ the omniscient narrator and two the first person observer. Two of the college pieces employ the omniscient narrator, one employs the first person observer, and three employ the central intelligence. A general shift from the omniscient narrator in the prep-school stories to the central intelligence in the college stories shows Fitzgerald's increasing concern with his characters' psychological reactions.

In "The Ordeal," "The Spire and the Gargoyle," and "Sentiment—and the Use of Rouge," conflict has been internalized. According to Percy Lubbock's *The Craft of Fiction* (as quoted in *The House of Fiction*), the "real actors" of the central intelligence method are the "thoughts, emotions and sensations" of the protagonist, and, according to Caroline Gordon and Allen Tate's *The House of Fiction*, the protagonist "is never off the stage and everything that happens is, in the end, referred to him and evaluated by him." (New York, 1960, p. 444) For instance, the opening paragraphs of "The Ordeal" convey an ever-narrowing focus: we see the Maryland countryside, a neighboring farmer, a lay-brother behind the monastery kitchen; our initial view of the young man comes through the eyes of the lay-brother, then shifts abruptly to an impersonal angle that becomes personal as the omniscient narrator enters the young man's mind, where, with the exception of two lines of dialogue at the end of Part I, he remains.

Fitzgerald was too subjective a writer to use this method well. Told basically from the point of view of the central intelligence, the protagonists of his two earliest novels often express immature ideas and emotions which he shares—a defect largely avoided in *Tender Is the Night* through a concealed narrator who provides sufficient detachment to control identification.

Meanwhile, Fitzgerald had perfected the first person observer technique. Here the storyteller is someone other than the author as author or character and so an aesthetic distance is created, which causes the author to consider not only his reactions but the reactions of the "persona" too. This accounts for the feeling of "objectivity" *The Great Gatsby* and *The Last Tycoon* manage to convey.

"The Mystery of the Raymond Mortgage" had introduced the first person observer, a method that may have been inspired by Edgar Allan Poe or Sir Arthur Conan Doyle. "The Room with the Green Blinds" was the only other prep-school story narrated from this point of view. As in the earlier story, the narrator participated passively without assimilating anything of importance and remained exclusively a reporter rather than a changing and growing character. Neither acquired anything of value and consequently neither matured. But such is not the case with the nephew of "The Pierian Springs and the Last Straw," for in the course of his experience, he learns a critical lesson.

There are a number of remarkable similarities between the nephew and Nick Carraway of *The Great Gatsby*. Both young men and both self-conscious observer-narrators, they share an upper-middle-class heritage, their families possessing firmly established roots and enough wealth to send male heirs to eastern schools. The nephew's father practices law and Nick's deals in wholesale hardware. Mr. Carraway advises his son, "Whenever you feel like criticizing any one, . . . just remember that all the people in this world haven't had the advantages that you've had," and the nephew's father acts the part of moral touchstone—conservative yet sympathetic—also: "Is that damn father of yours still defending me against your mother's tongue?" asks Uncle George. Like Nick's, the nephew's home town is a "prosperous Western city," although the initiatory journey of the story runs from east to west to east rather than from west to east to west. Finally, the nephew, who might have followed Uncle George's pattern ("your son here will be George the second"), learns through Uncle George's experience that artistic fulfillment may depend upon personal frustration, just as Nick Carraway learns through the experience of Jay Gatsby that older American values dictate abandoning Jordan Baker and the bond business.

The first person observer, the *homme manqué,* and the *femme fatale* developed throughout the apprentice fiction to reach their apex in "The Pierian Springs."

The Pierian Springs
and the Last Straw

My Uncle George assumed, during my childhood, almost legendary proportions. His name was never mentioned except in verbal italics. His published works lay in bright, interesting binding on the library table—forbidden to my whetted curiosity until I should reach the age of corruption. When one day I broke the orange lamp into a hundred shivers and glints of glass, it was in search of closer information concerning a late arrival among the books. I spent the afternoon in bed and for weeks could not play under the table because of maternal horror of severed arteries in hands and knees. But I had gotten my first idea of Uncle George—he was a tall, angular man with crooked arms. His opinion was founded upon the shape of the handwriting in which he had written "To you, my brother, with heartiest of futile hopes that you will enjoy and approve of this: George Rombert." After this unintelligible beginning whatever interest I had in the matter waned, as would have all my ideas of the author, had he not been a constant family topic.

When I was eleven I unwillingly listened to the first comprehensible discussion of him. I was figeting on a chair in barbarous punishment when a letter arrived and I noticed my father growing stern and formidable as he read it. Instinctively I knew it concerned Uncle George—and I was right.

"What's the matter Tom?—Some one sick?" asked my mother rather anxiously.

For answer father rose and handed her the letter and some newspaper clippings it had enclosed. When she had read it twice (for her naive curiosity could never resist a preliminary skim) she plunged—

"Why should she write to you and not to me?"

Father threw himself wearily on the sofa and arranged his long limbs decoratively.

"It's getting tiresome, isn't it? This is the third time he's become—involved." I started for I distinctively heard him add under his breath "Poor damn fool!"

"It's much more than tiresome," began my mother, "It's disgusting; a great strong man with money and talent and every reason to behave and get married (she implied that these words were synonymous) playing around with serious women like a silly, conceited college boy. You'd think it was a harmless game!"

Here I put in my word. I thought that perhaps my being *de trop* in the conversation might lead to an early release.

"I'm here," I volunteered.

"So I see," said father in the tones he used to intimidate other young lawyers downtown; so I sat there and listened respectfully while they plumbed the iniquitous depths.

"It is a game to him," said my father; "That's all part of his theory."

My mother sighed. "Mr. Sedgewick told me yesterday that his books had done inestimable harm to the spirit in which love is held in this country."

"Mr. Sedgewick wrote him a letter," remarked my father rather dryly, "and George sent him the book of Solomon by return post—"

"Don't joke, Thomas," said mother crowding her face with eyes, "George is treacherous, his mind is unhealthy—"

"And so would mine be, had you not snatched me passionately from his clutches—and your son here will be George the second, if he feeds on this sort of conversation at his age." So the curtain fell upon my Uncle George for the first time.

Scrappy and rough-pieced information on this increasingly engrossing topic fitted gradually into my consciousness in the next five years like the parts of a picture puzzle. Here is the finished portrait from the angle of seventeen years—Uncle George was a Romeo and a mesogamist, a combination of Byron, Don Juan, and Bernard Shaw, with a touch of Havelock Ellis for good measure. He was about thirty, had been engaged seven times and drank ever so much more than was good for him. His attitude towards women was the *piece-de-resistance* of his character. To put it mildly he was not an idealist. He had written a series of novels, all of them bitter, each of them with some woman as the principal character. Some of the women were bad. None of them were quite good. He picked a rather wierd selection of Lauras to play muse to his whimsical Petrarch; for he could write, write well.

He was the type of author that gets dozens of letters a week from solicitors, aged men and enthusiastic young women who tell him that he is "prostituting his art" and "wasting golden literary opportunities." As a matter of fact he wasn't. It was very conceivable that he might have written better despite his unpleasant range of subject, but what he had written had a huge vogue that strangely enough, consisted not of the usual devotees of prostitute art, the eager shopgirls and sentimental salesmen to whom he was accused of pandering, but of the academic and literary circles of the country. His shrewd tenderness with nature (that is, everything but the white race), his well drawn men and the particularly cynical sting to his wit gave him many adherents. He was ranked in the most staid and severe of reviews as a coming man. Long psychopathic stories and dull germanized novels were predicted of him by optimistic critics. At one time he was the Thomas Hardy of America and he was several times heralded as the Balzac of his century. He was accused of having the great American novel in his coat pocket trying to peddle it from publisher to publisher. But somehow neither matter nor style had improved, people accused him of not "living." His unmarried sister and he had an apartment where she sat greying year by year with one furtive hand on the bromo-seltzer and the other on the telephone receiver of frantic feminine telephone calls. For

George Rombert grew violently involved at least once a year. He
filled columns in the journals of society gossip. Oddly enough
most of his affairs were with debutantes—a fact which was considered particularly annoying by sheltering mothers. It seemed as
though he had the most serious way of talking the most outrageous nonsense and as he was most desirable from an economic
point of view, many essayed the perilous quest.

Though we had lived in the East since I had been a baby, it
was always understood that home meant the prosperous Western
city that still supported the roots of our family tree. When I was
twenty I went back for the first time and made my only acquaintance with United George.

I had dinner in the apartment with my aunt, a very brave,
gentle old lady who told me, rather proudly, I thought, that I
looked like George. I was shown his pictures from babyhood, in
every attitude; George at Andover, on the Y. M. C. A. committee,
strange anatomy; George at Williams in the center of the Literary
Magazine Picture, George as head of his fraternity. Then she
handed me a scrap-book containing accounts of his exploits and
all favorable criticism of his work.

"He cares nothing at all about all this," she explained. I admired and questioned, and remember thinking as I left the apartment to seek Uncle George at his club, that between my family's
depressed opinion of him and my aunts elated one my idea of
him was muddled to say the least. At the Iroquois Club I was
directed to the grill, and there standing in the doorway, I picked
one out of the crowd, who, I was immediately sure, was he. Here
is the way he looked at the time. He was tall with magnificent
iron grey hair and the pale soft skin of a boy, most remarkable in
a man of his mode of life. Drooping green eyes and a sneering
mouth complete my picture of his physical self. He was rather
drunk, for he had been at the Club all afternoon and for dinner,
but he was perfectly conscious of himself and the dulling of faculties was only perceivable in a very cautious walk and a crack in
his voice that sank it occasionally to a hoarse whisper. He was
talking to a table of men all in various stages of inebriation,

and holding them by a most peculiar and magnetic series of gestures. Right here I want to remark that this influence was not dependent so much upon a vivid physical personality but on a series of perfectly artificial mental tricks, his gestures, the peculiar range of his speaking voice, the suddenness and terseness of his remarks.

I watched him intently while my hall boy whispered to him and he walked slowly and consciously over to me to shake hands gravely and escort me to a small table. For an hour we talked of family things, of healths and deaths and births. I could not take my eyes off him. The blood-shot streakedness of his green eyes made me think of wierd color combinations in a child's paintbox. He had been looking bored for about ten minutes and my talk had been dwindling despondently down when suddenly he waved his hand as if to brush away a veil, and began to question me.

"Is that damn father of yours still defending me against your mother's tongue?"

I started, but strangely, felt no resentment.

"Because," he went on, "It's the only thing he ever did for me all his life. He's a terrible prig. I'd think it would drive you wild to have him in the house."

"Father feels very kindly toward you, sir," I said rather stiffly.

"Don't," he protested smiling. "Stick to veracity in your own family and don't bother to lie to me. I'm a totally black figure in your mind, I'm well aware. Am I not?"

"Well—you've—you've had a twenty years' history."

"Twenty years—hell—," said Uncle George. "Three years history and fifteen years aftermath."

"But your books—and all."

"Just aftermath, nothing but aftermath, my life stopped at twenty-one one night in October at sixteen minutes after ten. Do you want to hear about it? First I'll show you the heifer and then I'll take you upstairs and present you to the altar."

"I, you—if you—," I demurred feebly, for I was on fire to hear the story.

"Oh,—no trouble. I've done the story several times in books and life and around many a litered table. I have no delicacy any more—I lost that in the first smoke. This is the totally blackened heifer whom you're talking to now."

So he told me the story.

"You see it began Sophmore year—began most directly and most vividly in Christmas vacation of Sophmore year. Before that she'd always gone with a younger crowd—set, you young people call it now," he paused and clutched with mental fingers for tangible figures to express himself. "Her dancing, I guess, and beauty and the most direct, unprincipled personality I've ever come in contact with. When she wanted a boy there was no preliminary scouting among other girls for information, no sending out of tentative approaches meant to be retailed to him. There was the most direct attack by every faculty and gift that she possessed. She had no divergence of method—she just made you conscious to the highest degree that she was a girl"—he turned his eyes on me suddenly and asked:

"Is that enough—do you want a description of her eyes and hair and what she said?"

"No," I answered, "go on."

"Well, I went back to college an idealist, I built up a system of psychology in which dark ladies with alto voices and infinite possibilities floated through my days and nights. Of course we had the most frantic correspondence—each wrote ridiculous letters and sent ridiculous telegrams, told all our acquaintances about our flaming affair and—well you've been to college. All this is banal, I know. Here's an odd thing. All the time I was idealizing her to the last possibility, I was perfectly conscious that she was about the faultiest girl I'd ever met. She was selfish, conceited and uncontrolled and since these were my own faults I was doubly aware of them. Yet I never wanted to change her. Each fault was knit up with a sort of passionate energy that transcended it. Her selfishness made her play the game harder, her lack of control put me rather in awe of her and her conceit was punctuated by such delicious moments of remorse and self-denunciation that it

was almost—almost dear to me—Isn't this getting ridiculous? She
had the strongest effect on me. She made me want to do something for her, to get something to show her. Every honor in college took on the semblance of a presentable trophy."

He beckoned to a waiter to my infinite misgiving, for though
he seemed rather more sober than when I had arrived, he had
been drinking steadily and I knew my own position would be
embarrasing if he became altogether drunk.

"Then"—between sips—"we saw each other at sporadic inter-
vals, quarreled, kissed and quarreled again. We were equals, neither
was the leader. She was as interested in me as I was fascinated by
her. We were both terrifically jealous but there was little occasion to show it. Each of us had small affairs on the side but
merely as relaxations when the other was away. I didn't realize
it but my idealism was slowly waning—or increasing into love—
and rather a gentle sort of love." His face tightened. "This
isn't cup sentiment." I nodded and he went on; "Well, we broke
off in two hours and I was the weak one."

"Senior year I went to her school dance in New York, and
there was a man there from another college of whom I became
very jealous and not without cause. She and I had a few words
about it and half an hour later I walked out on the street in my
coat and hat, leaving behind the melancholy statement that I
was through for good. So far so good. If I'd gone back to college
that night or if I'd gone and gotten drunk or done almost anything wild or resentful the break would never have occurred—
she'd have written next day. Here's what did happen. I walked
along Fifth Avenue letting my imagination play on my sorrow,
really luxuriating in it. She'd never looked better than she had
that night, never; and I had never been so much in love. I worked
myself up to the highest pitch of emotional imagination and
moods grow real on me and then—Oh poor damn fool that I
was—am—will always be—I went back. Went back! Couldn't I
have known or seen—I knew her and myself—I could have plotted
out for anyone else or in a cool mood, for myself just what I
should have done, but my imagination made me go back, drove

me. Half a thought in my brain would have sent me to Williamstown or the Manhattan bar. Another half thought sent me back to her school. When I crossed the threshold it was sixteen minutes after ten. At that minute I stopped living."

"You can imagine the rest. She was angry at me for leaving, hadn't had time to brood and when she saw me come in she resolved to punish me. I swallowed it hook and bait and temporarily lost confidence, temper, poise, every single jot of individuality or attractiveness I had. I wandered around that ballroom like a wild man trying to get a word with her and when I did I finished the job. I begged, pled, almost wept. She had no use for me from that hour. At two o'clock I walked out of that school a beaten man."

"Why the rest—it's a long nightmare—letters with all the nerve gone out of them, wild imploring letters; long silences hoping she'd care; rumors of her other affairs. At first I used to be sad when people still linked me up with her, asked me for news of her but finally when it got around that she'd thrown me over people didn't ask me about her any more, they told me of her—crumbs to a dog. I wasn't the authority any more on my own work, for that's what she was—just what I'd read into her and brought out in her. That's the story—" He broke off suddenly and rose; tottering to his feet, his voice rose and rang through the deserted grill.

"I read history with a new viewpoint since I had known Cleopatra and Messaline and Montespan,"—he started toward the door.

"Where are you going?" I asked in alarm.

"We're going upstairs to meet the lady. She's a widow now for awhile so you must say Mrs.—see—Mrs."

We went upstairs, I carefully behind with hands ready to be outstretched should he fall. I felt particularly unhappy. The hardest man in the world to handle is one who is too sober to be vacillating and too drunk to be persuaded; and I had, strange to say, an idea that my Uncle was eminently a person to be followed.

We entered a large room. I couldn't describe it if my life depended on it. Uncle George nodded and beckoned to a woman at a bridge four across the room. She nodded and rising from the table walked slowly over. I started—naturally—

Here is my impression—a woman of thirty or a little under, dark, with intense physical magnetism and a most expressive mouth capable as I soon found out of the most remarkable change of expression by the slightest variance in facial geography. It was a mouth to be written to, but, though it could never have been called large, it could never have been crowded into a sonnet—I confess I have tried, Sonnet indeed! It contained the emotions of a drama and the history, I presume, of an epic. It was, as near as I can fathom, the eternal mouth. There were eyes also, brown, and a high warm coloring; but oh the mouth. . . .

I felt like a character in a Victorian romance. The little living groups scattered around seemed to move in small spotlights around us who were acting out a comedy "down stage." I was self-conscious about myself but purely physically so; I was merely a property; but I was very self-conscious for my Uncle. I dreaded the moment when he should lift his voice or overturn the table or kiss Mrs. Fulham bent dramatically back over his arm while the groups would start and stare. It was enormously unreal. I was introduced in a mumble and then forgotten.

"Tight again," remarked Mrs. Fulham.

My Uncle made no answer.

"Well, I'm having a heavy bridge game and we're ever so much behind. You can just have my dummy time. "Aren't you flattered?" She turned to me. "Your Uncle probably told you all about himself and me. He's behaving so badly this year. He used to be such a pathetic, innocent little boy and such a devil with the debutantes."

My Uncle broke in quickly with a rather grandiose air:

"That's sufficient I think Myra, for you."

"You're going to blame me again?" she asked in feigned astonishment. "As if I—"

"Don't—Don't," said my Uncle thickly. "Let one poor damn fool alone."

Here I found myself suddenly appreciating a sudden contrast. My Uncle's personality had dropped off him like a cloak. He was not the romantic figure of the grill, but a less sure, less attractive and somewhat contemptible individual. I had never seen personalities act like that before. Usually you either had one or you didn't. I wonder if I mean personality or temperament or perhaps that brunette alto tenor mood that lies on the borderland... At any rate my Uncle's mood was now that of a naughty boy to a stern aunt, almost that of a dog to his master.

"You know," said Mrs. Fulham, your Uncle is the only interesting thing in town. He's such a perfect fool."

Uncle George bowed his head and regarded the floor in a speculative manner. He smiled politely, if unhappily.

"That's your idea."

"He takes all his spite out on me."

My Uncle nodded, Mrs. Fulham's pardners called over to her that they had lost again and that the game was breaking up. She got rather angry.

"You know," she said coldly to Uncle George, "You stand there like a trained spaniel letting me say anything I want to you—Do you know what a pitiful thing you are?"

My Uncle had gone a dark red. Mrs. Fulham turned again to me.

"I've been talking to him like this for ten years—like this or not at all. He's my little lap dog. Here George, bring me my tea, write a book about me; you're snippy Georgie but interesting." Mrs. Fulham was rather carried away by the dramatic intensity of her own words and angered by George's unmovable acceptance. So she lost her head.

"You know," she said tensely, "My husband often wanted to horsewhip you but I've begged you off. He was very handy in the kennels and always said he could handle any kind of dog!"

Something had snapped. My Uncle rose, his eyes blazing. The shift of burden from her to her husband had lifted a weight from his shoulders. His eyes flashed but the words stored up for ten years came slow and measured.

"Your husband—Do you mean that crooked broker who kept

you for five years. Horsewhip me! That was the prattle he may
have used around the fireside to keep you under his dirty thumb.
By God, I'll horsewhip your next husband myself." His voice had
risen and the people were beginning to look up. A hush had fallen
on the room and his words echoed from fireplace to fireplace.

"He's the damn thief that robbed me of everything in this
hellish world."

He was shouting now. A few men drew near. Women shrank to
the corners. Mrs. Fulham stood perfectly still. Her face had gone
white but she was still sneering openly at him.

"What's this?" he picked up her hand. She tried to snatch it
away but he tightened his grip and twisting the wedding ring
off her finger he threw it on the floor and stamped it into a beaten
button of gold.

In a minute I had his arms held. She screamed and held up
her broken finger. The crowd closed around us.

In five minutes Uncle George and I were speeding homeward
in a taxi. Neither of us spoke; he sat staring straight before him,
his green eyes glittering in the dark. I left next morning after
breakfast.

*   *   *   *   *   *   *   *   *   *

The story ought to end here. My Uncle George should remain
with Mark Anthony and De Musset as a rather tragic semi-
genius, ruined by a woman. Unfortunately the play continues into
an inartistic sixth act where it topples over and descends like
Uncle George himself in one of his more inebriated states, con-
trary to all the rules of dramatic literature. One month afterward
Uncle George and Mrs. Fulham eloped in the most childish and
romantic manner the night before her marriage to the Honorable
Howard Bixby was to have taken place. Uncle George never
drank again, nor did he ever write or in fact do anything except
play a middling amount of golf and get comfortably bored with
his wife.

Mother still doubts and predicts gruesome fates for his wife,
Father is frankly astonished and not too pleased. In fact I rather

believe he enjoyed having an author in the family, even if his books did look a bit decadent on the library table. From time to time I receive subscription lists and invitations from Uncle George. I keep them for use in my new book on *Theories of Genius*. You see I claim that if Dante had ever won—but a hypothetical sixth act is just as untechnical as a real one.

Appendix: "The Death of My Father"

Edward Fitzgerald died of heart trouble during January, 1931. His son, who journeyed from Europe to Rockville, Maryland, to attend the funeral, fictionalized this event in *Tender Is the Night* (Charles Scribner's Sons, New York, 1953, p. 222):

> For an hour, tied up with his profound reaction to his father's death, the magnificent façade of the homeland, the harbor of New York, seemed all sad and glorious to Dick. . . .
>
> Next day at the churchyard his father was laid among a hundred Divers, Dorseys, and Hunters. It was very friendly leaving him there with all his relations around him. . . .
>
> "Good-bye, my father—good-bye, all my fathers."

But the demise of Edward Fitzgerald also inspired the remarkable document found among The F. Scott Fitzgerald Papers entitled "The Death of My Father," which, in turn, served a later literary use. According to Matthew J. Bruccoli, Sections #72 and #73 of *The Drunkard's Holiday*—an earlier draft of *Tender*—contain material from it, though most "was omitted before serialization" because these anecdotes were "distracting." (*The Composition of Tender Is the Night*, Pittsburgh, 1963, p. 123) The material included "the going for the papers together, the 'liar' argument, and the Civil War stories." (*Ibid.*, p. 125)

"The Death of My Father" is undated, written in pencil on faded ruled paper, and badly torn.

The Death of My Father

by Scott Fitzgerald

Convention would make me preface
this with an apology for the lack
of taste involved in discussing an
emotion so close to me. But all my criterions
of taste disappeared when reading Mrs
Emily Price Post's Book
of Etiquette some months ago.
Up to that time I had always thought myself
as an American Gentleman, perhaps
somewhat crazy and often desperate
but partaking of the sensitivity
of my race and class and
leaving behind me a record of
many times having injured the strong but never
the weak.
But now I don't know — the mixture
of the obvious and the snobbish in that book
— and its an honest book, a
frank piece of worldly wisdom
written for the new women of the
bull market — has set me back
even to all the things I felt at twenty. I kept
wondering all through it how Mrs
Post would have thought of my

(2)

my father.

I loved my father — always deep in
my subconscious I have referred judgementally
back to him, what he would
have thought, or done. This was
~~not~~ ~~because~~ ~~the~~ ~~love~~ ~~he~~ ~~caress~~
he loved me — and ~~felt~~ a
deep responsibility for me —
I was born several months
after the sudden death of my two elder
sisters + he ~~felt~~ ~~what~~ the effect of this
would ~~have be~~ on my mother, that
he would be my only
moral guide. No ~~knew~~ ~~felt~~
~~with her only~~ ~~my~~ became that
to the best of his ability. He came
from tired old stock with very ~~little left~~ ~~on the~~
of vitality and mental energy but he
managed to raise a little for me.
We ~~walked down town in the~~
Summer to have our shoes shined
me in my ~~socks~~ sailor suit and father
in his always beautifully cut
clothes and he told me the
few things I ever learned about
life until a ~~few~~ years later from

a catholic priest, Monsignor ~~Fay~~
What he knew he had learned from
his ~~father~~ mother & grandmother, the
latter ~~a~~ ~~before~~ used to me — "If your
grandmother Scott heard that she
would turn over in her grave."
What he told me were simple
things, ~~like~~

"Once when I went in a room as
a young man I was confused
said went up to the oldest woman
there and introduced myself and
afterwards the people of that town always
thought I had good manners" He did
that from a good heart that
came from another America
— he was much too sure of
what he was, much too sure of the
deep pride of ~~the two proud women~~ who brought
him up to doubt for a moment that ~~his own~~
~~instincts were part~~ — and it was
a horror to find the
natural gesture expressed
with every distortion he

and we bought the Sunday papers.

④

Mrs Price Post's book

We walked down town in Buffalo
on Sunday mornings & my white
ducks were stiff with starch & he was
very proud walking with his ~~little boy~~ handsome ~~boy~~
~~after~~ ~~a~~ ~~we~~ We had our shoes
shined and he lit his cigar. When
I was a little older I did not
understand at all why men that I
knew were vulgar and not gentlemen
made him stand up or give
the better chair on our verandah.
But I know now. There was new young
peasant stock coming up every ten years
& he was part of the ~~last~~
generation of the colonies ouf
the revolution.

Once he hit me. I called him a
liar — I was about thirteen I think
& I said if he called me a liar he was
a liar. He hit me — he had spanked
me before & always with good
reason but this time there was
ill feeling & we were both deeply

on which we violently agreed.

sorry for years I think though
we didn't say anything to
each other. Later we used to
have awful rows on the
political subjects but we
never came to the point of personal
animosity about them but things came
to [crossed out] ever the one most affected
quitted the arena, left the room.

[crossed out line] I don't [illegible] Mitten
[crossed out] the
[crossed out] debate

I ran away when I
was seven on the fourth
of July — I spent the day with
[crossed out] a friend in a pear orchard
& the police were informed that I
was missing and on my return
my father thrashed me according
to the custom of the nineties —
on the bottom and then [crossed out] let
me come out and watch the night
fireworks [crossed out] from the balcony.

with my pants still down +
my behind smarting - knowing
in my heart that he was absolutely
right. Afterwards, perhaps in
a ~~could be mood~~ - seeing in
his face his ~~first~~ regret that
it had to happen I asked him
to tell me a story. I knew what
it would be - he had only a few
the story of the Spy, the one about the Man
Hung by his Thumbs, the one
about Early March.

Do you want to hear
them. I'm so tired of them
all that I can't make them
interesting. But not they are because I
used to tell father to asked to
repeat, report.

Index

183